BDO LLP is the world's fifth large and accounting network, providing audit, tax and advisory services to start-ups, SMEs, and AIM-listed, FTSE-100 and multinational clients. In the UK, BDO is recognised as a leader in exceptional client service, with 3,600 staff in 18 offices, and 260 partners. Globally, the organisation operates in 162 countries, with over 74,000 people working out of 1,500 offices.

Daniel Dover is a senior partner at BDO LLP. He established the firm's Tax Investigations Group just over 30 years ago – now known as the Tax Dispute Resolution team. He is a recognised specialist in the area. Daniel's expertise covers all matters relating to the UK HMRC investigation office, including disputes involving questions of domicile and residence of both corporate and private entities. Daniel also advises businesses and families with their strategic direction. He is a trustee of a number of prominent charities and advises a wide range of charities on the tax pitfalls and governance issues they face. He is the co-author of *The Taxman Always Rings Twice*, *An Inspector Calls*, *An Inspector Returns*, *War or Peace* and *HMRC – Her Majesty's Roller Coaster*.

Helen Adams is a Principal in BDO LLP's Tax Dispute Resolution team, managing cases opened by HMRC's Fraud Investigation Service under Codes of Practice 8 and 9 (Contractual Disclosure Facility for suspected serious tax fraud). She also represents clients who want to voluntarily disclose tax irregularities to correct past years' tax positions; resolves complex local district enquiries (including tax-avoidance matters involving Accelerated Payment and Follower Notices); and advises on whether Alternative Dispute Resolution (mediation) may be a suitable way to resolve a tax enquiry. A contributing author to Bloomsbury Professional's *HMRC Investigations Handbook*, Helen regularly writes articles for various professional publications. She is a Vice Chair of the CIOT's Management of Taxes technical sub-committee and a member of its Tax Adviser editorial sub-committee.

Jonathan Pugh first studied law which presented him with hours of doodling practice. After a brief stint as an art teacher, he began his career as a freelance cartoonist in 1987. In January 2010 he joined the *Daily Mail* as their daily pocket cartoonist after nearly fifteen years at *The Times*. He was voted the Cartoon Art Trust Pocket Cartoonist of the Year in 1998, 2000, 2001, 2007 and 2010 and was the British Press Awards Cartoonist of the Year in 2001.

The New Face of HMRC

Behind the Tangled Web

Daniel Dover and Helen Adams

With cartoons by Pugh

P
PROFILE BOOKS

First published in Great Britain in 2018 by
Profile Books Ltd
3 Holford Yard
Bevin Way
London
WC1X 9HD
www.profilebooks.com

Copyright © BDO 2018
55 Baker Street
London
W1U 7EU
www.bdo.co.uk

The moral right of the authors has been asserted.

Copyright © cartoons by Pugh

All rights reserved. Without limiting the rights under copyright reserved above, no part of this publication may be reproduced, stored or introduced into a retrieval system, or transmitted, in any form or by any means (electronic, mechanical, photocopying, recording or otherwise), without the prior written permission of both the copyright owner and the publisher of this book.

A CIP record for this book can be obtained from the British Library

ISBN 978 1 78816 142 8
eISBN 978 1 78283 488 5

Designed and typeset by sue@lambledesign.demon.co.uk
Printed and bound by CPI Group (UK) Ltd, Croydon, CR0 4YY

While care has been taken to ensure the accuracy of the contents of this book, it is intended to provide general guidance only and does not constitute professional advice. The information contained in this book is based on the authors' understanding of legislation, regulation and practice at the time of publication, all of which is subject to change, possibly with retrospective effect. Neither they nor BDO LLP can therefore accept any legal or regulatory liability from readers acting on the information given.

Contents

	Acknowledgements	vii
	Foreword	ix
	In the beginning	xiii
	Introduction	xiv
1	Acceptable tax planning, unacceptable avoidance or evasion?	1
2	Information, information, information…	7
3	Exchanges of information	13
4	Whistleblowers	16
5	Voluntary disclosure	20
6	The taxpayer: individuals – domestic and foreign	24
7	The taxpayer: companies and businesses	28
8	The taxpayer: charities and trusts	34
9	The changing nature of the taxpayer	39
10	Professional advisers	44
11	The changing nature of HMRC	50
12	Tackling offshore non-compliance	57
13	Tackling tax avoidance	62
14	Compliance enquiries	68
15	Full-blown investigations	75

16	Criminal investigations	86
17	Legal procedures	91
18	Penalties	95
19	Tax debt management	102
20	The final destination	106

APPENDIX 1	Top ten tips	109
APPENDIX 2	Our ten favourite excuses	110
APPENDIX 3	Statutory Residence Test summary	112
APPENDIX 4	HMRC's taxpayer's charter	118
APPENDIX 5	Behaviours	119
APPENDIX 6	Penalties for offshore matters and offshore transfers	121

Glossary of acronyms (and more) — 123

Acknowledgements

We are grateful to many people for their help in the production of this book.

Firstly, to Helen Abrahams, whose considerable organisational ability kept us all in line and on track. Secondly, to Helen Dover, the world's leading expert at unravelling the intricate tales woven by her husband.

The drive and motivation behind us all came from Paul Eagland, the BDO UK Managing Partner. It was Paul who kick-started the process for producing the book. He promised to fire us with enthusiasm. Had we refused, he promised to fire us – with enthusiasm!

Our colleagues at BDO UK – Wendy Walton, Dawn Register, Richard Morley and Mark Sassoon, who encouraged and supported us all along the way.

Sincere thanks to Pugh, whose cartoons never fail to raise a wry smile, even among the driest denizens of HMRC. He excels at encapsulating a message in a direct but humorous manner. Special thanks go to our dear publisher Andrew Franklin and his wonderful team at Profile Books, for their contributions and support. Andrew considers himself 'a prince among men and peerless among equals'. With this publication, does he have a point?!

Last but not least we must acknowledge the role of HMRC in all this. Without them…

Daniel I. Dover and Helen Adams, July 2018

Foreword

This book is intended to give you, the reader, a taste of what life might be like should Her Majesty's Revenue and Customs (HMRC) decide that you've got your sums wrong and have, as a consequence, paid insufficient tax. It updates and adds to BDO's previous tome on the subject, *HMRC – Her Majesty's Roller Coaster: Hints on How to Survive a Tax Investigation*, a widely recognised work of genius published in 2014 and the fifth book in the series.

Since that date the tax world has changed almost beyond recognition. Dealing with the taxman has never been a bundle of joy (although taxpayers have been known to shout 'Hallelujah' when a settlement was in sight). But there were times when laughter was possible ... and useful as a safety valve. Nowadays those times are hard to come by. Governments are putting more and more pressure on HMRC to raise revenue and to prosecute greater numbers of tax evaders – especially those making use of offshore arrangements.

The leak of the so-called Panama Papers in 2016, and of the Paradise Papers a year later, revealed to an incredulous general public the extent to which privileged individuals and corporations with access to trusts and bank accounts in tucked-away places may avoid paying tax without breaking the law.

To help HMRC check whether it can gather more tax from these offshore avoiders, the government passed reams of new legislation and gave the agency powers that some believe take it into dangerously uncharted waters. The once-clear dividing line between what is legal, acceptable tax planning and what is not has become ever more blurred. Honest taxpayers (i.e. most of us) are no longer certain about what a fair tax bill looks like. Inevitably, more and more of us feel that we need advice – on the one hand, so we don't pay any more than we owe; on the other, so we don't become an object of interest to HMRC's sleuths.

A previous book in this series used the metaphor of a roller coaster to describe the experience of a tax investigation, suggesting some of the ups and downs that the experience entails. For this book we chose something darker to suit the change of times and the change of mood. A tax investigation, we suggest, has become akin to a spider's search for food. HMRC spins a web out of new legislation enacted by the government, as well as the information that it receives. The amount of that information increased dramatically in the year or so before this book was published, multiplying the strands of that web considerably, and with this expanded and reinforced web, HMRC aims to catch out errant taxpayers as they buzz around doing whatever they normally do.

Our aim in this book is to inject a little humour into the increasingly serious business of calculating and collecting tax. At the time of writing, our crystal ball has not cleared sufficiently for us to predict the effect of Brexit on the HMRC

investigations web, so things may be somewhat different by the time you read what follows.

This book also comes with a wealth warning. Whatever you do, don't go anywhere near the taxman's web without decent intelligence – far more of it than can be provided in this slim volume; the law is far more complex than these pages give us space to portray.

In the beginning

Who would have guessed 200 years ago that Sir Walter Scott's famous quote 'Oh what a tangled web we weave, when first we practise to deceive' would inspire the title of this book?

HMRC once declared that 'Tax doesn't have to be taxing', but things have changed as HMRC, taxpayers, investigations and the world around us have all become more complex. We therefore aim to show how HMRC currently uses its web of legislation and information to tackle the provision of disinformation – or no information – by errant taxpayers. To begin with, it is worth clarifying exactly what is meant by 'evasion', 'avoidance' and 'tax planning'.

Introduction

Ever since the Romans first introduced Britons to the idea of taxes, people have looked for ways to avoid paying them. Some of these ways have been legal and some of them have not. Those that were legal were generally called 'tax avoidance'; the rest were described as 'tax evasion'. Denis Healey, a former chancellor of the exchequer, once said that the difference between tax evasion and tax avoidance was 'the thickness of a prison wall'.

But nothing is that simple anymore (if it ever was). Quite the contrary. As HMRC fights a constant rear-guard action to close loopholes, many of them the unintended consequences of earlier legislation, so the rules become ever more opaque. HMRC now states that 'tax avoidance involves bending the rules of the tax system to gain a tax advantage that Parliament never intended ... It involves operating within the letter, but not the spirit, of the law.' In other words, some 'old-fashioned' tax avoidance may now be deemed unacceptable. The once-clear distinction between avoidance and evasion has, to some extent, disappeared.

In this new world, the taxpayer is left to interpret what Parliament intended. 'Read my lips, not just what is in Hansard' seems to be Westminster's new rule – an ironic echo, perhaps, of George Bush Sr's famous line on his presidential nomination in 1988: 'Read my lips: no new taxes.'

It is perfectly natural to feel aggrieved at the growing complexity of the rules. Nobody (well, almost nobody) minds paying their dues. At 5.7 per cent, Britain has one of the lowest tax gaps (the difference between what HMRC thinks it is owed and what is collected) in the world. But few Brits today feel they have the ability to calculate what those dues legitimately are as the rules are very complicated. Differing interpretations of the law are arguably one of the biggest causes of the tax gap, alongside evasion, 'criminal attacks' and failure to take reasonable care.

Left to their own devices to decide on what is right and proper, honest taxpayers do two things. Firstly, they turn increasingly to professional advisers. Secondly, in the absence of clear guidance, they rely on instinct and guesswork, neither of which is inclined to work in their – or HMRC's – favour.

HMRC's number-one objective now is to 'maximise revenues due and bear down on avoidance and evasion'. Little distinction is made between the two. Incidentally, if you google the phrase 'bear down' you will find two dictionary definitions. One (referring to a woman in labour) is to 'exert downwards pressure in order to push the baby out'. The other is to 'move quickly towards you in a threatening way', not unlike like what HGVs seem to do on motorways. Take your pick.

HMRC is now much more assertive in its pursuit of unpaid taxes, especially the offshore variety. It is literally telling taxpayers: 'Come to us before we come for you.' It is offering a number of 'confessionals' – routes whereby taxpayers can own up to previous misdemeanours without the full bite of the law snapping at their wallets.

At the heart of this new regime is what HMRC calls 'aggressive tax planning' – schemes promoted by tax planners to fulfil what Lord Justice Clyde deemed, in a famous tax case, to be the right of 'astute' taxpayers to pay no more than is honestly owed (*Ayrshire Pullman Motor Services v Inland Revenue*, 1929). Increasing numbers of these 'tax avoidance arrangements' (TAAs) are now considered to fall outside of what Parliament intended. As that happens, tax is being clawed back from people who (sometimes in all innocence, thinking they were an investment) used such schemes. At the same time,

measures are being introduced to discourage TAAs from being used in future, alongside a broad catch-all provision known as the General Anti-Abuse Rule (GAAR).

While HMRC is going after the schemes themselves, it is

also going after those promoters of the schemes whom it says 'exhibit certain behaviours' – a phrase that George Orwell would undoubtedly have enjoyed (although, of course, we are not for a moment suggesting that HMRC's world outlook is beginning to resemble *Animal Farm*).

All this is adding yet more to the piles of tax legislation already on the statute books. The UK tax code runs to almost 20,000 pages. That is many times the length of *War and Peace*, and far less exciting. Some are already saying that our tax law is spinning out of control, a tangled mess of incomprehensible detail. In 2010 the government was moved to set up the Office of Tax Simplification in order to identify areas where complexities might be reduced. If only it were that simple…

The government could perhaps learn a lesson from some of the spiders whose webs their legislation increasingly resembles. Webs lose their stickiness over time, so spiders simply chew up their old silk strands and recycle the protein in a new web. Maybe the 20,000 pages of the UK tax code could similarly be swallowed up and subsequently regurgitated at half the length. It would then perhaps gain greater stickiness and become more effective at catching the big-time tax evaders and avoiders who continue to slip through it.

CHAPTER 1

Acceptable tax planning, unacceptable avoidance or evasion?

Before we launch into our exploration of HMRC's web or the taxpayers it wants to trap within it, we need to understand the basics. What do we mean by tax evasion? Is it worse than tax avoidance? And what about tax planning, can we still do that?

For as long as tax legislation has existed, people have employed advisers to find the loopholes in it and reduce their tax bills. Directors are obliged by law to maximise company profits, and one way to do this is to minimise expenses, legally. Parliament expects this – indeed, it even helps sometimes. On other occasions, the results are not what Parliament wants, so law is added and the web expands.

Tax planning is legitimate. Gift aid, capital allowances, and research and development tax reliefs are, to name a few, examples of holes deliberately made in the HMRC tax web to encourage taxpayers to behave in certain ways. Even the transfer pricing and tax residence rules anticipate a certain level of tax planning as taxpayers arrange their tax affairs to minimise the money going to HMRC.

Tax laws are complicated. Many people, and almost all businesses, will need professional help from time to time to successfully navigate them – for example, when selling a business, expanding to trade overseas or moving to the UK. Much better to take and follow advice from a specialist than make mistakes trying to understand it yourself from the brief, simplified guidance on the internet.

A debate is now raging about what is acceptable tax planning and what is unacceptable avoidance. Where is the line, or indeed the edge of the web?

At times in the past, too much effort was expended trying to find holes in the web of legislation that the government never intended to exist, or trying to shoehorn things into these same holes. This was usually done by way of tax avoidance schemes – series of transactions that, when done in sequence, aimed to reduce or delay tax bills. They involved such things as film investments, used cars, second-hand watches and

manufactured dividends. The mantra of 'If it sounds too good to be true, it probably is' was forgotten. With hindsight, this was the face of what is now considered unacceptable tax avoidance.

The government wants the tax system to be fair and to fund 'essential' public services – otherwise voters start to feel aggrieved. UK businesses complain, too, if they are trying to play by the rules and consider their competitors are not doing likewise – the interaction of multi-jurisdiction tax rules used by multinational online businesses, for example, creates an uneven playing field. So the government continually reworks the tax rules to reduce taxpayers' and advisers' ability to avoid taxes, and to deter them from trying to do more, but there seems to be a limit to what can be achieved, particularly where borders are crossed.

Don't forget that some schemes were tax evasion, not avoidance, if tax returns were submitted relying on steps which did not actually happen (such as companies which were not incorporated when the loan was made or false diary

entries) – they stepped to the wrong side of the prison wall. In some evasion cases, prison cells awaited those professionals and their clients who should have known better.

So what is tax evasion? This occurs when a taxpayer

deliberately gives HMRC a document that he knows contains an error, with the intention that HMRC will rely on it as an accurate document. It also occurs when a person consciously chooses not to find out the correct position, despite knowing they should do so.

Examples include:

- Omitting interest from an overseas bank account from a tax return, despite it being taxable in the UK;
- Including too low a sales figure in accounts, reducing the profit and using the lower profit figure in the business's tax return;
- Creating false invoices to hide the diversion of funds into a private bank account, making them look like legitimate business expenses;
- Intentionally failing to register to pay tax; and
- Deliberately failing to submit tax returns.

Knowledge and intent are the crucial elements of evasion.

In summary – tax evasion involves deliberate actions to mislead HMRC. Tax avoidance that stretches the web in a way that Parliament never intended is usually unacceptable to HMRC. Tax planning is usually perfectly acceptable as long as it is implemented properly so that it meets all the rules. Saying that your company was set up and is run overseas, so is not taxable in the UK, is fine – as long as that is shown to be the reality.

Knowledge is power

We live in an information age, and HMRC is no exception to this – everything it does begins with information. It starts

spinning its web with data drawn from the UK and across the globe. It wants to know everything about everyone. It can then identify the evaders and avoiders to lure into its web for investigation.

CHAPTER 2

Information, information, information...

Retailers emphasise that business is all about 'location, location, location' – or at least they did so before the IT revolution enabled consumers to shop from home. For tax collectors, business is all about 'information, information, information'. Information is their life blood – the spun silk with which they weave their webs and try to trap their prey.

HMRC's web of powers includes information-gathering strands, such as requiring banks, employers and other businesses to provide it with data on interest earned, salaries and credit card sales. Promoters of some tax avoidance schemes are required to notify HMRC of their creation and use, thereby tipping off HMRC so it can decide whether to investigate further once those taxpayers' tax returns are submitted. Estate agencies, banks, advisers and many other businesses are required to alert law enforcement agencies via 'suspicious activity reports' if they suspect a customer is financing terrorism or laundering money – these provide a useful prompt for HMRC to consider opening investigations.

HMRC can ask taxpayers nicely to provide information for its enquiries – or arrive on their doorstep unannounced with

a formal notice. Third parties, such as customers, suppliers, rental agents and local planning authorities, may be formally required to help HMRC with its enquiries into other people, too.

In the olden days, information-gathering was a matter of reading newspapers, watching TV and keeping your ears open, especially in places like pubs and golf clubs – places where men are prone to boast of their fiscal dexterity. And magazines like *Private Eye* and *Vanity Fair* sometimes did an excellent job as HMRC sleuths.

In today's digital world, by contrast, information is byte-sized. Not only are there online registers of the owners of super-yachts and private jets, there are apps like Google Streetview to reveal the size of people's homes and the cars on their drive. There is also a digital dimension to the eternal clash between prudence and human vanity. The likes of Facebook, LinkedIn, Instagram and Twitter provide endless opportunities for tax evaders and avoiders to go public inadvertently with evidence of their misdeeds – or for their so-called friends to do it for them.

At the same time, the internet has become a key means of communication for HMRC itself, the interface between tax officials and the general public. The days when the elegantly phrased final demand was hand-written in a spidery scrawl and delivered by a real live postman are now numbered as the online 'personal tax account' becomes business as usual.

The government is investing over a billion pounds 'to transform HMRC into one of the most digitally advanced tax administrations in the world,' says the tax authority, thus 'finishing the delivery of our multi-channel digital services so we become a "digital-by-default" organisation.' Taxpayers would be well advised to become digital by default, too.

The idea of privacy and social media seems like an oxymoron

these days. HMRC has declared that it 'may observe, monitor, record and retain internet data which is available to anyone. This ... includes news reports, internet sites, Companies House and Land Registry records, blogs and social networking sites where no privacy settings have been applied.'

Conversely, HMRC will share your personal data with third parties where it is permitted by law, in the public interest or necessary for the performance of HMRC or other government departments' duties. It may share it with overseas tax authorities. Within the UK, HMRC can share data with the police, courts, debt collection and credit reference agencies, to name a few. It can also obtain information from other government bodies such as the Land Registry and UK Border Agency, an organisation that can tell it when people enter and leave the country – very useful when checking someone's residence.

However, information is not like motherhood or apple pie – an unquestionable good. There is a downside to it. As HMRC's net trawls in more and more of it, is there perhaps a danger that the great big spider at the centre of it all will become less and less able to digest it (the Panama and Paradise Papers between them consisted of approximately 25 million documents)? Given advances in data analysis, perhaps digestion will improve as the 'bytes' increase.

All this information is spun into the HMRC as HMRC uploads it onto its 'Connect' system. This system helps HMRC's officers draw connections between data from a myriad of domestic government and corporate sources to create a profile of what each taxpayer's total income, expenses and wealth might be, and to detect any relationship networks that may be otherwise invisible. (An escort agency was allegedly uncovered by Connect after it matched a string of credit card transactions with a large private residence owned by a person with apparently little income. HMRC duly taxed the profits.)

The Connect system is fully operational ... and having an effect. In December 2016, HMRC sent out 10,000 so-called nudge letters (letters worded to nudge people into taking a certain course of action) to individuals who had completed their 2014/15 returns. The letters asked them to look again at the amount of interest they had declared. Discrepancies were flagged for further investigation when Connect compared tax returns with information received from banks and other financial institutions. To misquote E. M. Forster: 'Only Connect the tax returns and the bank accounts, and guess which will become more exalted.'

CHAPTER 3

Exchanges of information

It has long been obvious that high-level tax evasion and avoidance are international activities in need of an international solution. Their central *modus operandi* is the channelling of funds into offshore jurisdictions where taxes are lower, information sharing is rarer, and questions are fewer.

Many of these jurisdictions are in sunny climates – the likes of Panama, Monaco and the Seychelles. Not all of these places, however, are a long-distance flight away. Places like Monaco and Luxembourg are within the EU, while Jersey, Guernsey and the Isle of Man are actually British Crown Dependencies. Moreover, full-sized sovereign states like Ireland, the Netherlands and Switzerland have legislation that makes them attractive low-tax bases for certain non-residents.

Most of these places offer taxpayers more accommodating legal and fiscal jurisdictions than they can find on the British mainland. The Isle of Man, for example, imposes no capital gains or inheritance tax on its residents, some of whom may consider that to be fair compensation for the isolation of the place and the noise of motorcycles.

For years, many offshore havens managed to remain outside

the spreading international network of what are known as Tax Information Exchange Agreements (TIEAs). International pressure, however, gradually persuaded many of them to share their data across borders. This is often in response to specific requests – the UK will ask an overseas country to source information on its behalf, and vice versa. If criminal tax evasion or money laundering is suspected, criminal law information exchange kicks in, and documents and computers may be seized and sent back in the diplomatic baggage.

Then there is a veritable tsunami of information fast approaching our shores annually. After 30 September 2018, something called the Common Reporting Standard (CRS) will be fully effective in the UK. From that date, financial institutions in over 100 different jurisdictions will be compelled to pass to their tax authorities certain information about the income of customers who are resident in other countries. The tax authorities of the participating jurisdictions then share this information with any overseas authority with which the customer is associated. More than half of the participating jurisdictions started to exchange such information in September 2017.

Once the CRS is fully functioning, the taxman will inevitably be swamped with zillions of terabytes (it even sounds like something out of a horror movie). This might slow down HMRC's ability to assess the tax due in more complicated cases – even with the help of Connect and extended assessment time limits.

Unsurprisingly, some people are looking for ways to dodge the CRS web. The UK and EU will legislate for mandatory disclosure of cross-border arrangements with specific characteristics, including arrangements designed to avoid CRS disclosure and to render offshore structures opaque. Deliberately

moving assets to avoid the CRS can be expensive if it triggers an offshore asset moves penalty.

Taxpayers concealing income and gains in opaque offshore arrangements and on remote sandy islands should note that the chances of being discovered are increasing sharply. They also need to note what options they have if they wish to minimise the penalties that may be imposed for their past misdemeanours.

CHAPTER 4

Whistleblowers

Lots of data comes to the taxman's attention thanks to whistleblowers, people who break through the bounds of confidentiality to pass information to the authorities directly or indirectly. The most widely publicised tax information to emerge in recent years is not something that was extracted by HMRC, but rather the vast volumes of data disclosed to journalists as the Panama Papers and the Paradise Papers.

Since as long ago as 1890, HMRC has been entitled to reward whistleblowers for their efforts. Each year the taxman pays hundreds of thousands of pounds to them – although only a few of the 100,000 whistleblowers that report to HMRC each year get rewarded. Nowadays there is a special phone line for them to call (0800 788 887) and a website that they can visit: www.gov.uk/government/organisations/hm-revenue-customs/contact/reporting-tax-evasion.

Most whistleblowers are not on the Panama Papers scale, and many are happy to tell their tales for nothing. Their motivations can be complex. Some believe that righteous behaviour is its own reward; others are rewarded by the consequent discomfort of their cheating neighbours (or former partners);

while for yet others, it's all about Me. They are trying to do a deal – 'if I tell you about Fred and Sarah will you let *me* off?'

HMRC reports that the majority of people who disclose the tax affairs of others are former work colleagues or bitter ex-wives and ex-husbands. Former spouses can be particularly enthusiastic whistleblowers. In the words of one tax officer, 'divorcees know where the bodies are buried'. They take the attitude that if their ex is going to do without them, then he (and it is usually a 'he') is going to do without a lot of other things besides. To chess enthusiasts this is known as the BDO – the Bitter Divorcee's Opening!

But beware. Whistleblowing is not always the rewarding experience it might be imagined to be. When a former HSBC systems-engineer-turned-whistleblower was interviewed by a journalist in France in 2013, he felt the need to wear an artificial beard and to be accompanied by three bodyguards. The whistleblower responsible for what became known as LuxLeaks, the exposure of Luxembourg's secret sweetheart deals with multinationals, received a prison sentence and a fine. None of the corporations or politicians involved in the deals were even censured.

Following the leaking of the Panama Papers, the UK government set up a special taskforce involving HMRC and other national agencies to look into the leaked information and to take action on any wrongdoings that it might uncover.

In addition, HMRC was given a 'briefcase' of new powers that add several sturdy strands to its web. The powers introduced a whole new swathe of acronyms to HMRC's already acronym-rich vocabulary (see the glossary on page 123, specially designed for those readers who might, at this stage in the proceedings, be said to be 'losing the thread'.)

CHAPTER 5

Voluntary disclosure

HMRC prefers to get information direct from taxpayers rather than indirectly via whistleblowers, so it is always keen to persuade taxpayers to tell the whole truth. And now, with its new improved bite, HMRC is keener than ever to persuade taxpayers to come clean and to set their record straight. Experience has taught it that giving taxpayers a fair chance to correct past mistakes can be a cost-effective way of collecting unpaid tax.

Under this regime, those who get in there first (before they are nudged or tapped on the shoulder for investigation) often get brownie points in the form of reduced penalties. The taxman has set up a number of channels for taxpayers to make voluntary disclosures about past underpayments of tax without being subject to a full investigation, including via its Digital Disclosure Service. This should not be confused with a procedure called 'voluntary restitution', whereby HMRC asks taxpayers to pay taxes that they have failed to pay in the past, even though there is no strict legal obligation to do so. In such cases, no interest is charged for the late payment. Few avail themselves of this 'facility'!

Much of HMRC's efforts are focused on offshore 'non-compliance'. A series of 'disclosure facilities' culminating in the Worldwide Disclosure Facility (WDF) in 2016 acts as a sort of confessional, giving UK taxpayers with assets in foreign countries a standard, relatively 'light touch' process with some protection from prosecution if they come clean. Taxpayers register their wish to make use of the facility (they can do so online), and they then have a certain period of time in which to lay out their past misdemeanours.

A more recent piece of legislation (the so-called Requirement to Correct, RTC) required taxpayers who made past errors in their UK tax returns relating to offshore affairs to correct them before 30 September 2018 ... or else. Failure to do so could result in a serious 'correctional' procedure – including demands for payment of up to 300 per cent of the undeclared tax, for instance, plus further penalties and general publication of the details of the case, thus 'naming and shaming' the perpetrators.

The message of the WDF and the RTC is clear: this is the taxpayer's final chance to correct past UK tax returns before HMRC examines the zillions of terabytes that flood its way from the Common Reporting Standard (CRS). A word of warning here. These bytes could cause a nasty bite to many an errant taxpayer.

The targets: taxpayers

Speaking about taxpayers, let's look at who they are in a little more detail...

CHAPTER 6

The taxpayer: individuals – domestic and foreign

The key yardstick for tax liability in the UK is the concept of residence. A person who 'resides' in a particular country becomes liable to its taxes. (In the United States the key yardstick is nationality. Generally, anyone with an American passport or a green card is liable to American taxes on all of their worldwide income, regardless of where they live, where their income arises and where they choose to keep it.)

You can be resident in more than one country at the same time. Through bilateral treaties and various multilateral agreements, the jurisdictions involved decide among themselves how to share the dual-resident's dues. It is an old-established principle that taxing the same income twice ('double taxation' – either in different geographical entities or in different legal entities) is to be avoided wherever possible. No fly should be devoured in two different webs.

There is, however, a new conundrum over residence that taxpayers need to watch out for. Scotland and Wales are both independently introducing tax rules that diverge from those of the rest of the UK, so individuals must consider which part of the UK they reside in, but since there is free movement of labour throughout the UK, this is bound to create problems for tax officers. Some 80,000 Brits move in or out of Scotland each year – some of them without informing HMRC of their change of address. Collecting what each of them owes in different places is a difficult task.

UK residence is determined by the number of days that a person spends in the country. Before April 2013 it was quite simple. If a person slept in the UK for fewer than 90 nights in any one year, then he or she was deemed to be non-resident. There were special rules for people like airline pilots and cabin crews, people who spent much of their time working in the air, a space that has not (yet) been claimed by any tax authority. But in recent years the rules have become more complicated (see Appendix 3, page 112). It is now possible for someone to be deemed resident despite only spending 16 days of the year in the UK, depending on their other ties to the UK. Once a UK resident, a person is taxable on their worldwide income and gains, unless 'domicile' comes to their aid.

The UK is sometimes seen as a tax haven for the super-rich because it allows a very peculiar creature to wander its tax web with greater freedom than its usual residents. This creature is known as a 'non-dom'. Non-doms are people who are resident in the UK (a large percentage of them live in London), but who are deemed to be 'domiciled' elsewhere. 'Domicile' is a changeable concept that depends on factors such as a person's father's domicile when they were a child, the location of their permanent home, and the place where they state they intend to remain indefinitely. A person's domicile can alter several times during their life, so HMRC usually requires voluminous evidence to support a person being domiciled outside the UK.

Typically, non-doms are people who were born overseas

and moved to the UK sometime later, perhaps posted to a job in London for a number of years. They are taxed on their overseas income and capital gains only to the extent that they remit them to the UK. This is known as the 'remittance basis' of taxation. Care is always needed with constructive (indirect) remittances such as paying UK expenses using a credit card paid from an offshore account. They are only constructive in that they increase the tax payable!

In the eyes of Joe Public, however, the archetypal non-dom is a Russian oligarch whose home is a football pitch's distance from Belgrave Square, or an Arab sheikh living within a muezzin's call of Marble Arch. Most of these people's income arises abroad and, not surprisingly, they like to spend it before it passes over the White Cliffs of Dover, preferably while lounging on a super-yacht moored in the South of France.

For the bona fide non-dom, there was a time when HMRC's web was like Teflon, a surface onto which not much stuck. But the non-dom's privileges have been whittled away drastically in recent years. Firstly, once they had been in the UK for seven years, non-doms could only lay claim to the remittance basis if they paid an annual lump sum to HMRC. Then the government declared that it wanted no one who had lived in the UK for at least 15 of the last 20 years to be able to claim the remittance basis. Now rules for those who became non-UK domiciled before returning here are being tightened, too.

Residents who feel that they might be able to escape from the UK's tax web by moving abroad will not find the process easy. And even when they establish themselves as non-resident to HMRC's satisfaction, they may still find themselves the object of arachnidism from HMRC. The UK taxes properties held by non-residents or through offshore structures in several ways, including via capital gains tax (CGT), inheritance tax (IHT) and the Annual Tax on Enveloped Dwellings (ATED).

Residence, domicile and remittances are high on HMRC's list of neon warning signs for further scrutiny. When profiling, HMRC would also be well advised to focus to a greater degree on small and medium-sized businesses (SMEs), including the self-employed. HMRC estimates that they accounted for approximately 53 per cent of the country's tax gap for 2016/17. Particularly prone to making mistakes are fast-growing start-ups, characterised by a lack of internal procedures and governance. One taxpayer, who used his start-up business as a piggy bank, lived at a top London hotel, ate out every night, and charged all the expenses of his lifestyle to the company. Until, one day, he suddenly felt the suffocating sensation of the taxman's web closing in…

CHAPTER 7

The taxpayer: companies and businesses

While arachnophobic individuals scour the planet for places beyond the taxman's web, HMRC is turning its attention more and more to some of the greatest beneficiaries of the largesse of tax havens – global corporations. Big multinational businesses are alleged to dodge paying up to £9.6 billion a year in taxes.

But HMRC is struggling to get its fangs into these big operators, who can shift in and out of different jurisdictions almost at will. A powerful committee of MPs went so far as to accuse HMRC of losing its nerve 'when it comes to mounting prosecutions against multinational corporations', although of course not even HMRC can mount a prosecution against someone who has not committed a crime.

Companies like Amazon, Google, Apple and Facebook are perceived to pay very little tax on their profits anywhere. Popular discontent erupts occasionally against these giants; the public sees them as gaining an unfair competitive advantage over their smaller rivals by using complex offshore tax arrangements. This is particularly evident in the coffee-shop business, where many enterprising small operators around the country have to compete with big tax avoiders like Starbucks, which succumbed to public pressure in 2013 and voluntarily paid over £20 million to HMRC.

In 2015, in a measure designed to extract more tax from these big boys, the UK introduced a so-called Diverted Profits Tax (DPT). This imposes a 25 per cent tax on groups deemed to be artificially shifting profits overseas. The stated aim is to 'counter the use of aggressive tax-planning techniques by multinational enterprises to divert profits from the UK to low-tax jurisdictions.'

The first DPT was paid in 2017, and the legislation was said to be influential in persuading online retailer Amazon to record sales made to its UK customers in the books of its UK branch rather than in low-tax Luxembourg.

Overall, companies are in a different position to individuals when it comes to avoiding tax. Their primary obligation is to their shareholders – to keep costs down and profits up – and tax can be seen as just another cost. As long as the basis for corporation tax is corporate profit, companies will be tempted to minimise the tax they pay by shifting profit whenever they can away from high-tax jurisdictions to low-tax ones – a practice known as base erosion and profit shifting (BEPS).

One way to expose this practice is by finding discrepancies between a company's profits and its turnover in different jurisdictions. A new OECD ruling states that companies with an annual turnover greater than 750 million must publish an annual breakdown of their turnover, profit, employees and tax paid, country by country. UK companies must send a copy of their country-by-country reports to HMRC, where they are likely to be pored over by Connect and HMRC officers.

A series of landmark cases starting in 1981 (known as the *Ramsey* cases) clarified that any tax avoidance scheme that lacked 'a business purpose' other than to save tax would be struck down. The tax due would be calculated as if the scheme were not in place. In 2013 a Supreme Court judge, Lord Walker, stated that since the Ramsey cases 'there has been an increasingly strong and general recognition that artificial tax avoidance is a social evil which puts an unfair burden on the shoulders of those who do not adopt such measures.'

To flush out more of it, the law is trying to align more closely the responsibilities of the corporation with those of the individual. In companies with a turnover greater than £200 million there must now be an employee with the title of Senior Accounting Officer (SAO); the SAO must vouch to HMRC that the company has appropriate accounting arrangements to allow its tax liabilities to be calculated accurately. Should the company be found to lack suitable arrangements, then the SAO may be fined £5,000. HMRC conducts business risk reviews periodically to identify those on which it needs to focus more closely. Large companies are required to publish their 'tax strategy' online and undertake country-by-country reporting.

Likewise, since September 2017 a company (or partnership) can be held liable for failing to prevent the facilitation of tax evasion (be it in the UK or abroad) by any one of its associates – this can be an employee or a supplier of goods and services. These new corporate criminal offences can be punished by unlimited fines.

Smaller companies that cannot afford the complicated offshore structures needed to escape from HMRC's web look for other ways to artificially reduce their profits, and hence their tax bills. Sometimes this means they incorporate and try to run their business overseas while making profits in the UK, arguing that they are resident or are permanently established elsewhere, so owe no UK tax.

Others try to reduce their tax bill by evasion, padding out their payroll with fictitious employees. Having come across workers called D. Duck, M. Mouse and Bert Einstein, however, HMRC has developed a keen eye for such subterfuge.

Another way for companies to escape the taxman's web was cut off in 2017. Under 'disguised remuneration packages', employees' pay could previously be diverted into an employee benefit trust (EBT), which granted them loans in its place, allowing them to avoid paying PAYE and National Insurance contributions (or so they hoped). HMRC now has powers to tax these packages as if they were straightforward pay.

The owners of a building business who had set up an EBT received a letter from HMRC after the trust had been running for several years. The letter offered them a 'settlement opportunity' to unwind the arrangement. After being released from HMRC's web, the builders realised that paying themselves straightforward salaries from the very beginning would have left them better off.

In another swipe at corporate avoidance, in 2016 HMRC launched the Offshore Property Developers Task Force to investigate whether offshore companies that develop properties in the UK have paid all their taxes. The aim is to put them on a level fiscal playing field with UK-resident companies in the same business.

People will go to great lengths to conceal the (often

considerable) gains from property deals. In one example, a taxpayer fell out with his business partner and a commercial dispute between them ended up in the high court. In the court's ruling, the judge asked if they were both up to date with their tax returns. This triggered HMRC's interest, and it transpired that the client had an Andorran bank account in his wife's name with several million dollars in it. He claimed the money was a gift. The person who gifted it to him was the person who had developed properties for him in the UK, properties that were not in his name. The case remains unresolved.

To try and reduce these sorts of issues, the government has said that it will introduce a public register showing who controls overseas companies that own UK property or participate in UK government procurement. The first of its kind in the world, the register is unlikely to go live before 2021.

CHAPTER 8

The taxpayer: charities and trusts

For a long time now, trusts have been used as a means to shelter income and capital gains from tax. The trust has been described as the basic building block of Anglo-Saxon secrecy. It has much the same effect on tax officers as places like Andorra and the British Virgin Islands: it makes them want to check what is going on so they can be sure that it has not created a great big hole in their web.

In recent years, charitable trusts were increasingly used as vehicles for tax avoidance and evasion, putting HMRC on especially high alert wherever they appeared. Mistakes in gift aid, particularly involving donations to attend fundraising dinners, proved expensive. UK charities donating to registered overseas charities must scrutinise those charities' activities to ensure their donations are properly used for charitable purposes. Failure to do so may result in the donations being deemed UK taxable income. Nowadays the taxman has little reticence when it comes to ensuring that charities pay their fair whack. Perhaps HMRC has a new motto: 'Charity begins with the Exchequer.'

However, there is still a perfectly valid reason for using

other types of trusts – to protect the assets of minors. Examples include ring-fencing assets against future divorces, or for allowing one beneficiary to enjoy an income from a bunch of assets while the assets themselves are preserved for future generations.

There is a wide variety of different trusts (including, for example, discretionary trusts, interest-in-possession trusts and bare trusts), each with its own set of tax rules. Anyone who puts property into a UK trust – any kind of trust – is obliged to inform HMRC of the fact. The trust's trustees must then file self-assessment tax returns to report any income or capital gain.

Many countries maintain registers of the beneficial ownership of their companies and trusts. Some of them require that information be made public. Companies House holds the UK's public register of what it calls 'People with Significant Control' – very useful for tax investigations. The 2018

Sanctions and Anti-Money Laundering Act authorised the UK government to compel all of Britain's Overseas Territories to set up public registers of the beneficial owners of companies based there by 2021 – that includes places like Bermuda and the Cayman Islands.

Since June 2017 the UK has had a national register of trusts. The register includes trusts that are resident in the UK for tax purposes. Trusts resident outside the UK that have a UK connection – such as a UK resident/domiciled settlor or beneficiary, or an underlying asset or income in the UK on which tax is payable – may require registration.

Foreign trusts – those where some or all of the trustees are not resident in the UK – are created overseas. They may be the tip of the iceberg – owning overseas companies that may link into the UK, owning property or investments here. Consequently, they may trigger tax charges under complex anti-avoidance rules. UK beneficiaries of foreign trusts must be especially careful and should seek expert advice. In one case, a family assumed they were receiving their inheritance from a relative's death estate with no tax due, but HMRC declared that the payments from the trust and home provided were taxable in the UK.

The taxman finds certain forms of foreign legal entities particularly confusing. Things like *stiftungs*, *anstalts* and *foundations* are rare specimens for HMRC to inspect. For UK tax they may feature a mixture of characteristics of companies and trusts. They make it difficult for outsiders to find out who are the true beneficiaries of the assets that they hold, and what the tax bill should be.

Finally, the key thing with a trust is to check that it really is just that. Did the settlor really intend to lose control of the assets when he moved them into the trust? Is the trust an illusion or a sham, effectively a personal piggy bank? If so, the settlor may well be taxable on the trust's income and gains as if they were their own.

Everything changes... nothing stays the same

Taxpayers are changing; HMRC is changing. Advisers are changing too – adapting to their clients' needs and the web of regulation spun by HMRC and the government.

CHAPTER 9

The changing nature of the taxpayer

At the turn of the twenty-first century, certain (fairly predictable) types of people were generally more accident prone than average with regard to their tax affairs. Cash deposit boxes, shoeboxes under the bed, false invoices, two sets of accounting records – one for the taxman and one for everyone else – were the usual hallmarks of such people's activities. Business types under scrutiny often included taxi drivers, takeaway vendors, market traders, second-hand-car salesmen, diamond dealers and gang masters. Some companies adopted triple entry bookkeeping: 'debit, credit and shred it.' While such examples persist, times, technology and the opportunities for tax mistakes march on.

Major economic and social changes inevitably have significant fiscal implications – for example, the shift of the labour market to the so-called gig economy, characterised by a prevalence of short-term contracts and freelance work. It is a market typified in the eyes of the general public by the city taxi service Uber.

Much attention is now paid to the fact that freelancers in the gig economy miss out on holiday pay, sick leave and rules regarding the minimum wage. On the other hand, such people are left to their own devices when it comes to calculating their tax. There is no employer automatically deducting PAYE and National Insurance contributions from their pay. Like all self-employed people, they must declare their income and calculate their own expenses for tax purposes. This can provide scope for some imaginative weaving and they, perhaps somewhat inevitably, sometimes get stuck.

Every year HMRC publishes a list of some of the items that more brazen taxpayers have tried to claim as expenses. One individual claimed £4.50 for a meal of sausage and chips. Nothing peculiar in that, you might say, except for the fact that they claimed it 250 times in the same year. And another taxpayer claimed the vet fees for a rabbit. (The taxman, of course, told him to go and get stuffed.)

HMRC is keen to narrow the tax gap between full-time employees and self-employed people in the gig economy. In a test case at the beginning of 2018, a freelance BBC presenter was deemed to be a full-time employee and ordered to pay over £400,000 in back tax. At about the same time, the European Court of Justice ruled that a UK window salesman who worked full-time on a self-employed basis for the same company for 13 years was entitled to holiday pay.

Another recent change in the taxpayer's way of life with serious fiscal implications lies in the increasing globalisation of employment. In the first half of the last century, few taxpayers earned income abroad. During the second half of that century, the nature of work changed. Nowadays, actors, sports stars, architects and even engineers travel the world with their skills and earn income from all over the place. Both their country of residence and the country where they do their work have an interest in the tax arising from that income.

The modern-day taxpayer's shopping habits also have fiscal implications. More and more goods and services (almost a quarter of all fashion items, and up to 50 per cent of all printed books sold in the UK) are now purchased online, and the nature of these transactions makes it easier to avoid paying VAT. HMRC wants to make the online market-places themselves – the likes of Amazon – more responsible for the unpaid VAT of their vendors. It recently signed an agreement with the two big digital superstores to access their data in its fight against VAT evasion by overseas online retailers.

For some time, vendors have had to display a VAT number on their websites. In March 2018 HMRC took this a step further, announcing that if sellers (whether based in the UK or overseas) do not pay the correct VAT when selling into the UK, and are not removed from the site following the issue of a notice by HMRC to the market-place, then HMRC will pursue the market-places themselves for any future unpaid tax due from those sellers.

HMRC is also looking to see if information technology could enable it to collect VAT directly from these web markets before the vendors themselves fly away with the funds.

People selling goods via websites like eBay without declaring the money they make may not be doing anything wrong if they are just selling personal belongings of relatively low value. Others believe they are employed and do not realise they became part of the 'hidden economy' by not declaring the proceeds of their trading activities. Websites like Airbnb make it easy to rent out your home for a few weeks a year, but the consequences are the same as if you were renting to a tennis player at Wimbledon ... tax is due on the rent. HMRC can use its information powers to obtain details of your activities from the website and will extrapolate your profits so it can assess and demand payment for the tax due. Penalties will be sure to follow, too.

Finally, we live in an ageing society in which ever greater wealth is accumulating in the hands of the elderly. So HMRC is finding that an increasing number of taxpayers who come under investigation are frail and hard of hearing. Such people are not subjected to heavy interrogation by HMRC, but their affairs are not exempt from investigation. Tax officers have heard many old wives' tales that turned out to be just that.

CHAPTER 10

Professional advisers

Anybody who is being investigated by HMRC will soon find that they need support – in the form of a reputable adviser who can pick his or her way through the tangled web of tax law (and who also knows HMRC's *modus operandi* well enough to provide moral support). The taxman's web may look harmless enough from a distance, but once you get up close and personal, and see all the hirsute detail, it can be a very different matter. Hairy can be really scary.

It is definitely not a good idea to look for support from old Tommy whom you met this morning on the 8.43 creeping from Crawley, who told you he was in the City and knew how to 'spin the tax chappie a yarn'. Still less to follow the golf club gossip or hotel bar chatter.

Serious advisers are obliged to keep up to date with changing tax law and to follow a code drawn up by the Institute of Chartered Accountants in England and Wales, alongside a number of other regulatory bodies. Called Professional Conduct in Relation to Taxation (PCRT), it sets out standards of behaviour that all members of these associations must follow. The latest version of the code addresses issues around the promotion of tax avoidance in particular.

A professional adviser can be a source of technical knowledge in an era when HMRC has increasingly high expectations of the taxpayer's own knowledge of the ever more complicated tax code. An adviser can also be a font of sound practical advice, based on the fact that they have almost certainly seen it all before (see our top ten tips in Appendix 1, page 109). On occasions, advisers can even be a shoulder to cry on. (Indeed, taxpayers have been known to judge them on the quality of their tea and sympathy – and of their biscuits.)

Initially, advisers may seem expensive. But they can ultimately save their clients a good deal of money – usually far more than their bills. In extreme cases they may even manage to keep their clients out of jail.

One of the biggest benefits of having an adviser is the frequent communication that he or she has with HMRC. Advisers spend their lives dealing with tax officers. If anyone understands these spidery creatures and their behaviour, they do. HMRC has even begun to ask advisers to do some of their work for them – for instance, asking them to send out letters to appropriate clients announcing that HMRC will shortly be receiving information on overseas financial accounts, and advising such clients to check that their tax affairs are in order.

As far as HMRC is concerned, a taxpayer can choose to be represented professionally at any stage in any proceedings. And taxpayers are free to change advisers in mid-investigation.

Some of what is disclosed to an adviser is covered by the law on privilege. But a case that went all the way to the Supreme Court confirmed that not all of it is. For example, a client who is seeking accountancy advice 'in contemplation of litigation' may claim privilege only for those documents that were created with the prospect of that litigation in mind. It is always best to check with an adviser at the very beginning of a relationship what is and what is not covered by privilege. As with all tax rules, do not assume that the law is going to be the same as it was when last you asked about it.

Of course advisers, like taxpayers, come in many forms. HMRC is all too aware of this. Indeed, vibrations along its

> **Regimes HMRC may use to sanction professional advisers**
>
> (**Dishonest tax agents** – tax agents who deliberately act with a view to bringing about a loss of tax.)
>
> **Promoters of Tax Avoidance Schemes (POTAS)** – sanctions promoters of schemes via a system of conduct and monitoring notices.
>
> **Enablers of Tax Avoidance Schemes** – sanctions promoters and other enablers of failed abusive tax avoidance schemes.
>
> **Enablers of Offshore Tax Evasion or Non-Compliance** – sanctions third parties who encourage, assist or otherwise facilitate the taxpayer to declare insufficient income tax, CGT or IHT in relation to offshore activities, despite the enabler knowing that their actions would or were likely to enable the evasion or non-compliance.

web have taught it that while most advisers are helpful to both taxpayers and HMRC, a small number are not, so HMRC are casting new skeins of silk to entangle them, too. Advisers who promote artificial schemes designed to reduce their clients' tax bills are targeted by the government, as are those who enable offshore tax evasion. HMRC wants to deter advisers from getting it wrong, so the consequences of being caught in these webs are severe, with fines and public exposure.

Under the Criminal Finances Act 2017, professional-services firms may be guilty of a criminal offence if an employee or associate fails to prevent the criminal facilitation of another person's tax evasion. An offence will be considered to have been committed even if the senior management of the business is not aware of what was going on. However, if managers have put in place what are described as 'reasonable prevention procedures', the firm itself should avoid prosecution. These new rules are designed to prevent businesses turning a blind eye to the under-the-counter activities of their staff and other representatives.

Incidentally, it is not just banks and professional services firms that are affected by these new rules – all businesses need to take some action. The level required will depend on the nature and scale of the business.

CHAPTER 11

The changing nature of HMRC

Tax officers, too, have changed in recent years, along with their job. Whereas they once were a bit like harmless daddy long-legs, going about their collecting business in a sometimes creepy-crawly way, but without the venom to enforce their will, these days they are armed with new legislation that gives them real bite. Modern tax officers are more black widow than daddy long-legs.

The Panama and Paradise Papers gave the general public a clearer idea of the lengths to which some high-profile figures will go to escape paying tax, legally or otherwise. These revelations put pressure on HMRC to tackle offenders, at more or less the same time as it became easier for it to do so, principally because it was given more resources and lots more data.

HMRC's web gives it considerable investigation powers. In extreme cases HMRC can apply for the authority to use surveillance powers. It can also force witnesses to answer questions or provide documentation under the Serious Organised Crime and Police Act 2005. In civil cases any officer can give written notice requiring a taxpayer to provide information or produce documents needed to check their tax position, and that includes all electronic documents, such as emails.

HMRC has long faced media accusations that it has been prepared to do 'sweetheart deals' with specially favoured customers, both corporate and individual. To counter these claims it issued what it called its Litigation and Settlement Strategy (LSS) and its Code of Governance for Resolving Tax Disputes. These are designed to bring stricter procedures and greater consistency to the resolution of differences of opinion with taxpayers. The net result: far more rigid adherence to technical criteria in disputes and less scope for negotiation.

HMRC is streamlining its operations into 20 or fewer offices.

The changing nature of HMRC

These will house all its operations covering companies, owner-managed businesses and individuals' self-assessment and other taxes. Its principal investigative team is the Fraud Investigation Service (FIS), dealing with civil and criminal cases, including organised crime. In addition, there are a number of other specialist departments, besides the one set up to deal with high-net-worth individuals (HNWIs). These cover areas such as trusts, inheritance tax, pension schemes, share asset valuations and capital gains.

The Birmingham-based Offshore Coordination Unit (OCU) was set up to manage the information that HMRC regularly receives from sources around the globe. The unit's head once claimed that it has to manage 80 times more data than the British Library. And that was before the CRS came into effect, trawling in regular information on bank accounts held in around 100 different jurisdictions overseas. It oversees the WDF but passes cases for investigation to other parts of HMRC, including the FIS.

Tax officers still do some old-fashioned sleuthing – noticing, for instance, expensive holiday rentals on the Cornish Riviera (most holiday rentals are advertised in magazines or on the internet) or making test purchases from takeaway vendors. They have a keen eye for inconsistencies between reality and the information that is provided in tax returns.

But on the whole, these days the taxman is relying more on information technology and less on shoe leather, and not just for sleuthing. For example, HMRC recently started texting late payers, having found SMS messaging to be a particularly effective form of reminder. It is also rolling out a programme called Making Tax Digital (MTD), which will have all firms with an annual turnover of more than £85,000 filing VAT returns digitally by April 2019.

It is HMRC's ambition to become 'the world's most digitally advanced tax authority'. That makes it more important for its officers to develop their computer skills than to further the talents that traditionally appeared in their job descriptions – talents such as good negotiating skills and powers of persuasion.

As technology evolves, HMRC will need to consider yet further changes to the tax system. Is taxing business profits acceptable or, given internet businesses, should there be a tax based on digital sales instead? How will cryptocurrencies be taxed? Are they a chargeable asset, providing trading profits, gambling or a means of payment like cash? And how should robots be taxed?

HMRC has also said that it is dipping its toe into artificial intelligence (AI). It is aiming to have automated 10 million processes by the end of 2018 and, at the same time, to be using robots to search out tax fraud. It has a £100 million computer that co-ordinates information from many different government and commercial databases, including information on individuals' credit-card transactions and their internet usage. Armed with this information, it estimates an individual's probable earnings and then compares them with their tax declarations, to see whether the computer 'thinks' they may be hiding something.

There are some general concerns about the implications of algorithm-based decision-making and whether it may, in some contexts, exaggerate and propagate social and racial prejudice. In the tax context, will it quickly adapt to new types of tax frauds and new ways of doing business?

Another recent change in HMRC was driven by its need to keep abreast of the increasing globalisation of the average taxpayer. Not only do UK taxpayers buzz around different webs as they work at home and abroad, but they also increasingly come from abroad. And they speak different languages.

But they should not imagine that this gives them free rein to discuss their illicit tax affairs in front of tax officers, who also increasingly speak foreign languages. If they do not speak your particular dialect of Malagasy, they will not hesitate to call in an interpreter who does.

Tax officers are also always highly skilled at understanding unspoken languages – the way in which taxpayers phrase their correspondence, for instance, or their body language when they attend meetings. If you look as if you have the weight of the world on your shoulders, then in all likelihood it is because you have. Likewise, people who are consistently shifty-eyed usually are so for a reason.

It is not wise, either, to assume that tax officers have an unbounded sense of humour, despite them regularly publishing a list of ridiculous excuses given for missing tax returns (see Appendix 2, page 110). One taxpayer, when asked in a questionnaire if they had 'any other income', chose to answer 'F All'. They were saved from being despatched to that web from which few escape by explaining that they had meant it to stand for 'Family Allowance'.

The investigatory web

So, HMRC's capabilities in terms of data analysis and powers to collect the 'right amount of tax' have arguably never been greater. Its web is the biggest and stickiest it has ever been. Let's talk about what they do with it.

CHAPTER 12

Tackling offshore non-compliance

Brits in search of a low-tax venue in which to park their assets (and/or themselves) need to choose their destination with care. In December 2017 the EU issued a blacklist of nine countries that it defined as 'uncooperative jurisdictions'. These countries' tax regimes, it said, 'facilitate offshore structures that attract profits without any real economic activity'.

The EU also issued a (much longer) grey list of 62 countries (including some British Overseas Territories, such as Bermuda

HMRC's web of measures for tackling offshore non-compliance

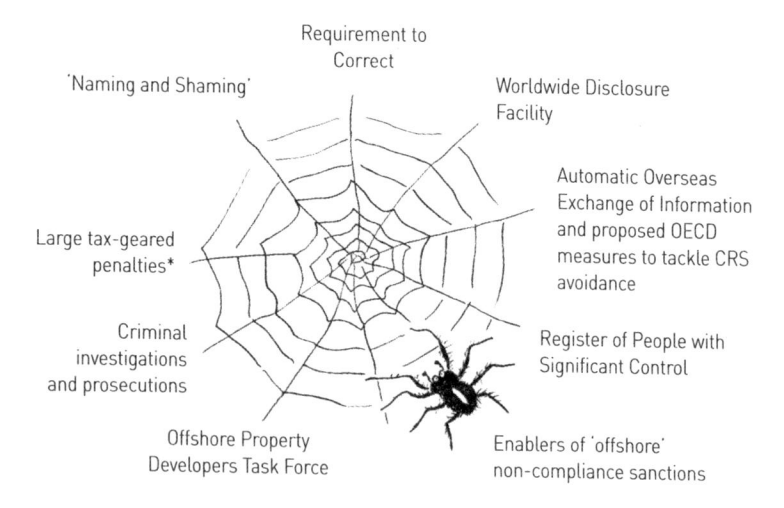

- Requirement to Correct
- 'Naming and Shaming'
- Worldwide Disclosure Facility
- Automatic Overseas Exchange of Information and proposed OECD measures to tackle CRS avoidance
- Large tax-geared penalties*
- Criminal investigations and prosecutions
- Register of People with Significant Control
- Offshore Property Developers Task Force
- Enablers of 'offshore' non-compliance sanctions

*Penalties can be up to 200% of the tax plus an offshore asset moves penalty of up to 100% plus a 10% asset value-based penalty

and the Cayman Islands) that it is observing, waiting to see if they fulfil promises they have made to change their tax rules.

Taxpayers who think they can outsmart HMRC by shifting assets to a country so they will not register through the CRS system will, if discovered, be subject to even heavier penalties than those who make no such move (through the ponderously titled offshore asset moves penalty).

HMRC's No Safe Havens strategy defines offshore evasion as 'using another jurisdiction's systems with the objective of evading UK tax'. It wants:

- There to be 'no jurisdictions where UK taxpayers feel safe to hide their income and assets from HMRC';
- Would-be offshore evaders to 'realise that the balance of risk is against them' (i.e. HMRC will find them);
- Offshore evaders to 'voluntarily pay the tax due and remain compliant';
- To detect evaders who do not come forward unprompted and impose 'vigorously enforced sanctions';
- There to be 'no places for the facilitators, or enablers of offshore tax evasion'.

HMRC's FIS and Offshore Coordination Unit are in the front line of HMRC's efforts to tackle offshore non-compliance. Non-compliance is everything from evasion, through avoidance, to tax planning that's gone wrong – or just plain mistakes. HMRC will use any of the tools at its disposal to tackle these issues: information powers, enquiries, full-blown investigations and criminal investigations with a view to prosecution.

The key issue for HMRC is evidence. The sort of evidence needed varies, depending on what is under investigation: an offshore bank account held by a UK resident, remittances from a non-UK domiciled person, whether a company is based in the UK, whether UK tax is due despite the use of an offshore trust ... the list goes on. It is critical to get lots and lots of evidence – ideally records made or kept by third parties rather than the taxpayer's memory – in order to answer questions like: What has the target done every day since he said he left the UK – and did he really leave?

The introduction of free movement within the EU made it more difficult for HMRC to establish how many days taxpayers spent within the confines of their web. As travellers cross EU borders, their passports are rarely stamped, so there is no formal record of their entry or exit. However, other traces of their travels are left behind. Mobile-phone and credit-card records, for example, can be a giveaway. While HMRC will investigate, the taxpayer should take care to keep their records, too – if it ends up in court, the burden of proving the case usually falls on the taxpayer.

Sailors who spend long periods abroad often come home with their pockets full of cash, hoping to avoid leaving a credit-card trail. But tax officers have a special sensitivity to cash. Large dollops of the stuff have always looked suspicious, perhaps like the unlaundered proceeds of a bank robbery. In the age of ubiquitous credit cards and online banking, there are fewer and fewer legitimate reasons for anyone to hold a stash of cash. Many tax officers assume that the only things it is used for are terrorism, arms and drugs. In any case, holding on to hard cash is a risky way to avoid leaving a trace of your movements. For one thing, it is highly inflammable and subject to theft. Large amounts also tend to show up in scanners at airports and such places.

As a result, some people in the criminal world are starting to use cryptocurrencies – digital stores of value, such as Bitcoin, that are exchanged without the intermediation of a bank. Their two biggest perceived advantages are that they are as yet unregulated, and they allow purchases to be made anonymously. The government has said, optimistically perhaps, that it will bring these virtual currencies into its anti-money-laundering regulations. What one person seeks to hide, another person will seek to find!

Once the taxman's net closes in on the unsuspecting taxpayer who thinks all is well because he took advice, things can get pretty sticky. Taking advice is all very well, as long as it is diligently followed. For offshore matters, this can be tricky – sometimes things get lost in translation and money ends up in the wrong bank accounts.

If mistakes were made and more tax is due, HMRC will try to issue discovery assessments to collect tax for multiple years – how many generally depends on why things went wrong. After that, as night follows day, late payment interest and penalties follow (see Appendix 6, page 121). Taxpayers who fail to cough up in relation to their offshore assets before 30 September 2018 face particularly steep penalties. They may be as much as 300 per cent of the tax, plus a 10 per cent asset-based penalty on top.

CHAPTER 13

Tackling tax avoidance

HMRC is casting its web wide to tackle tax avoidance, and it has many tools at its disposal to force avoiders into that web. It wants to shine a light on shadowy tax avoidance schemes, too. It does this by publishing 'spotlights' on its website – details of tax planning it considers unacceptable and ineffective – so as to dazzle the taxpayers and deter them from further planning of this type.

Additional deterrence comes from requiring the disclosure of certain types of tax planning to HMRC up front through DOTAS. HMRC is then on alert and its Counter-Avoidance Directorate (CAD) can decide whether to investigate immediately. Do not forget DOTAS either – this can be expensive as it gives HMRC a lot more time to issue its discovery assessment, and may lead to more penalties for the promoter of the scheme.

In addition to changing the detailed rules on when and how tax is charged, the government also introduced a General Anti-Abuse Rule (GAAR). This is a large net that HMRC can wield if permitted by the GAAR Advisory Panel. Any schemes that are caught by the GAAR net are defeated – tax is payable

HMRC's web of measures for tackling tax avoidance

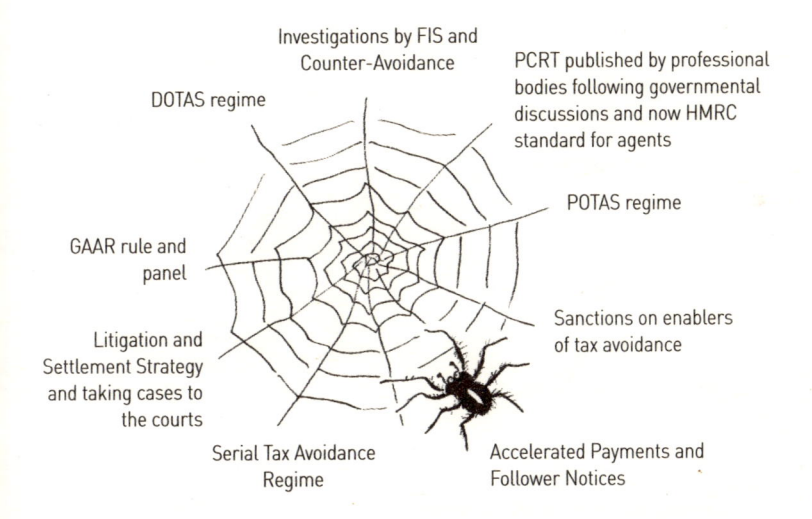

- Investigations by FIS and Counter-Avoidance
- DOTAS regime
- PCRT published by professional bodies following governmental discussions and now HMRC standard for agents
- POTAS regime
- GAAR rule and panel
- Sanctions on enablers of tax avoidance
- Litigation and Settlement Strategy and taking cases to the courts
- Serial Tax Avoidance Regime
- Accelerated Payments and Follower Notices

as if the arrangements never happened – and a large GAAR penalty may be charged, too.

The government had become frustrated with how long it took to tackle tax schemes through the courts following multiple appeals, even though HMRC wins over three quarters of these cases, while the taxpayer keeps hold of their money. Admittedly, HMRC chooses the cases it wants to litigate, so there is an inherent bias in these statistics. Accelerated Payment Notices (APNs) now force taxpayers to pay the tax that HMRC claims is attributable to the tax advantage they have gained from a scheme, even if an enquiry or appeal is unresolved. Failing to pay by the deadline results in APN penalties.

One taxpayer who received an APN for half a million pounds related to an investment he believed to be legitimate

Tackling tax avoidance

had a lucky escape. An enquiry into his return had been made 12 years earlier, but he had believed the matter closed. In the intervening 12 years he had retired, bought a holiday home in Spain and set about spending his pension pot. In the event, his advisers were able to demonstrate that HMRC had messed up their enquiry procedures. The taxpayer was given a lengthy time to repay, a gesture that saved him from bankruptcy.

As if the APN and GAAR additions to HMRC's tax avoidance web were not enough, Follower Notices (FNs) were added too. FNs force taxpayers to give up their challenges and accept court decisions that similar schemes do not work. There are some concerns that these new powers are retrospective and may come to deny taxpayers reasonable access to justice, especially since there is no direct right of appeal against either an APN or an FN, just the opportunity to ask HMRC to think again. Most judicial reviews (JRs) are costly and unsuccessful in the courts.

Penalties for defeated tax avoidance arrangements

GAAR penalties – 60% of the tax the scheme was intended to save.

APN penalties – total 5, 10 or 15% of the unpaid tax, depending on how late payment is made.

FN penalties – up to 50% of the tax that the scheme aimed to save or defer.

Penalties for errors – tax-geared penalties of up to 100% of the tax as shown in the graph on page 98, although they may be increased by offshore uplifts if the conditions are right.

Double jeopardy and other rules may mitigate these penalties somewhat, but others may be charged too, e.g. standard late filing and late payment penalties. The devil is in the detail...

On top of this, HMRC is always able to charge penalties for mistakes in tax returns. It could be a mistake to use an avoidance scheme – particularly if the steps taken went wrong even after professional advice. Advice is ignored for failed

---

Serial Tax Avoidance Regime (STAR)

HMRC will issue a **warning notice** within 90 days of a 'relevant defeat' of a tax avoidance arrangement. A 'relevant defeat' occurs when

- A GAAR counteraction notice becomes final;
- A Follower Notice is complied with or becomes final; or
- DOTAS (or the VAT equivalent) arrangements are counteracted, e.g. via closure notice, assessment or contract settlement.

The warning notice marks the beginning of a five-year **warning period** within which the taxpayer must submit information notices annually to HMRC. These notify HMRC of any new TAAs used in the period. If an information notice is submitted late or is wrong, the warning period starts again.

If during the warning period the taxpayer uses new TAAs that are subsequently defeated, then HMRC may charge **STAR penalties** of 20 to 60% of the tax 'saved' or deferred by the TAA.

If during the warning period the taxpayer uses three or more TAAs that are subsequently defeated, then HMRC may restrict the taxpayer's ability to claim some tax reliefs in future and/or publish the taxpayer's details publicly as a serial tax avoider.

schemes used after autumn 2017 so they will, in any case, be deemed careless.

Now HMRC is reaching for the stars with a new regime to penalise taxpayers where a scheme is defeated, even if this happens when a taxpayer voluntarily decides to give up their tax saving in order not to pay out for further appeals in court. Its STAR is triggered when it defeats a tax avoidance scheme. This keeps potential 'repeat' avoiders stuck in HMRC's web for some time, in the hope that they learn not to avoid again.

The sticky web of tax avoidance sanctions is most unappealing to potential purchasers of businesses, and giving up voluntarily is therefore often an attractive alternative – escaping the web before selling a business or stepping into the public eye is important. HMRC's spider is now rubbing its many hands as a result, but don't expect a deal. It is obliged to treat everyone the same – the full tax and late payment interest is payable, with penalties – resulting from HMRC's Code of Governance and LSS.

It is not just the users of TAAs that HMRC is going after. It is also cracking down on the promoters and enablers of such schemes, through POTAS and Enablers of Avoidance rules. If a scheme is defeated, then the enablers of that scheme may also find themselves subject to penalties.

CHAPTER 14

Compliance enquiries

HMRC's web of measures for tackling onshore (i.e. UK) non-compliance

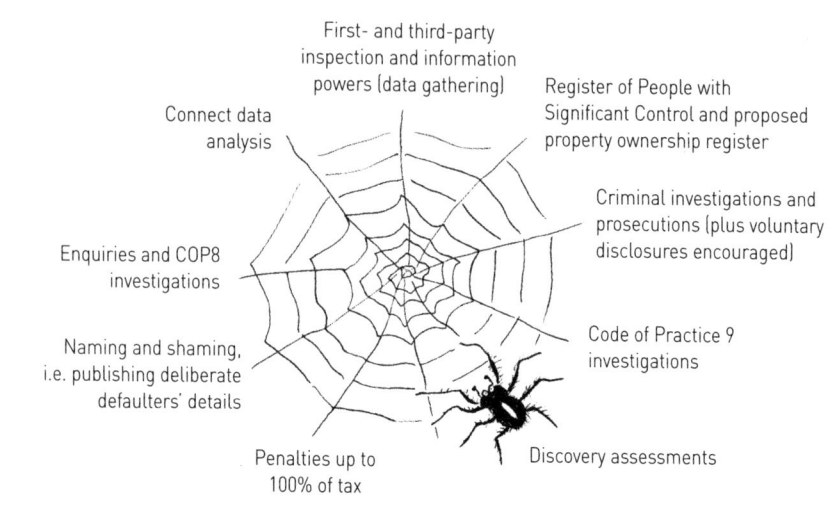

- First- and third-party inspection and information powers (data gathering)
- Register of People with Significant Control and proposed property ownership register
- Connect data analysis
- Criminal investigations and prosecutions (plus voluntary disclosures encouraged)
- Enquiries and COP8 investigations
- Code of Practice 9 investigations
- Naming and shaming, i.e. publishing deliberate defaulters' details
- Discovery assessments
- Penalties up to 100% of tax

HMRC considers enquiries to be an important way to tackle non-compliance – it initiates formal tax enquiries when it does not understand or agree with the position taken by a taxpayer.

Hot topics for enquiries

Income tax and CGT
- Residence, domicile, remittances and short-term business visitors
- Rental income
- Principal private residence exemption
- Tax avoidance arrangements

Inheritance tax
- Transferable nil-rate band and lifetime gifts
- Property valuations and joint ownership
- Business/Agricultural Property Relief claims
- Discounted gift trusts

Corporation tax
- Transfer pricing/diverted profits tax
- Corporate residence and permanent establishment
- Capital allowances
- Deductibility of expenses

Employer compliance
- Termination payments
- Employment status: employed v self-employed
- IR35/diversion of earnings
- Benefits in kind

VAT
- Late VAT registration
- Exempt v standard rated supplies v partial exemption
- Missing trader VAT fraud
- Lack of evidence for, or incorrect recovery of, input VAT

They usually concern one year's tax return only and, for the most part, have to be started within 12 months of the filing of the return. The starting gun is a letter from HMRC telling the taxpayer that their return is being scrutinised. The enquiry is then conducted primarily by correspondence.

Central to any enquiry is a determination of the facts of the case. But facts are fickle things. One senior tax official has said that 'a fact is a point of view unless both sides agree or the Tribunal affirms. This leads us to establish facts by proof, to prove things with evidence and to use information to persuade the enquirer of the existence of a fact.'

It is not a good idea to destroy evidence. Copies of things – digital and otherwise – have a nasty habit of proving indestructible at crucial moments. Tax officers will accept a number of excuses for lost documents and the late filing of returns, but 'the wife's pet spider ate it' is not one of them. Nor, in this digital age, is it possible to claim that 'a virus devoured my emails'. Most are retrievable with relatively little difficulty.

In any case, evidence can be your best friend. Keeping copious documents (electronic or paper) can provide the basis to disprove HMRC's assessments or persuade them that there is not a problem in the first place. Not all evidence is equal, though. Documents created by third parties such as banks and airlines are more likely to be accepted as evidence than your own memories or your diary (who deletes meetings when they do not happen?).

Lying about the facts of a case is not always a matter of what is said; it can be a matter of what is not said. When the famous jockey Lester Piggott reached a settlement with HMRC for not paying his taxes, he sent them a cheque drawn on an account that had never been disclosed. Piggott subsequently went to jail.

Thinking you can fob off a tax officer by giving only partial information is not a good idea either. HMRC does not take silence as an answer and will often issue a formal notice demanding information that it considers is reasonably required if you ignore their initial request. Delay can be expensive – if a formal information notice is issued, you are likely to be charged higher penalties if errors are subsequently found (see Chapter 18).

Once HMRC begins to look into an individual taxpayer's affairs it may look into everything. It can carry out a 'means review' that will pry into the most intimate details of a taxpayer's life, beginning with bank statements, credit-card statements, mortgage applications and the like. It searches to see how the taxpayer affords his lifestyle given the level of income declared. Appearing on TV programmes or online saying how wonderfully exotic your lifestyle is, then declaring very little income, is almost guaranteed to result in HMRC becoming intimately acquainted with your finances.

Even at this stage there is rarely any need for the taxpayer to meet HMRC directly. Most of the time, contact via the adviser is sufficient, usually by letter although meetings between the adviser and HMRC can occur periodically – they are often an effective way of working collaboratively with HMRC to resolve the dispute as envisaged by HMRC's LSS.

However, when it checks up on businesses, HMRC likes to visit their premises. Most business tax checks involve a visit by the VAT, employer compliance or corporation tax officers, sometimes all at once. Their aim is to better understand your business, review the records and identify any issues to look at in more detail. Usually this is all arranged well in advance, so you have plenty of warning.

If taxpayers of any type find themselves with a pre-arranged visit or in a meeting with HMRC then there are a few tips worth noting:

- Never lie to the taxman.
- Only answer the officer's questions. If you don't know the answer, don't try and guess. Just say, 'I don't know' or 'I can't remember'. It is allowed.
- Ensure there is a room ready for the visit and that the records requested are available – well organised, ready and waiting.

- Be kind and offer some basic refreshments – a three-course dinner with good wine is not necessary and may cause suspicion. Champagne lunches are out.
- Ensure your staff do not disturb HMRC at work, and do not gossip.
- Ask for an agenda in advance of the meeting.
- Make sure your adviser is there with you during the meeting.
- Stay calm. If you need a break, take one. HMRC do allow comfort breaks.
- Take notes, and if HMRC sends minutes of the meeting, check them against your notes. At times, things are misheard or misconstrued. Correcting them is essential.

Sometimes, during an enquiry into a self-assessment return, it becomes obvious to HMRC that the same issue has arisen in earlier years – a discovery! The tax officer will then set about assessing and collecting tax due for all the years in question. HMRC's powers in this area are extensive but not without limit. HMRC may assess up to 20 years of past tax (sometimes longer, if inheritances are involved), depending on the behaviour that caused the mistake. They also presume that the mistake occurred in earlier years, unless there is evidence to the contrary. Late payment interest will be charged and penalties may also be due.

Another HMRC tactic is to try to 'break' the accounting records – in other words, to discredit them entirely. This is sometimes done by comparing the taxpayer's income and expenses to 'norms' anticipated by HMRC for the same business type, extrapolating likely profits based on test purchases and combining these findings with the results of the means review. HMRC's aim is to justify assessing more tax for as many years as possible.

Once an enquiry is open, it is indefinite until HMRC decides, or the Tribunal (at the taxpayer's request) tells it to make up its mind. Most enquiries end with the issuance of a closure notice, a formal document from HMRC declaring (in the case of a 'final' closure notice) that it has closed an enquiry for good, or (in the case of a 'partial' closure notice) that it has closed its enquiries into one or more specific issues. Others may remain outstanding.

After receiving a final closure notice, a taxpayer cannot be quizzed about the same things again in respect of the same periods – unless HMRC becomes aware that the facts of the matter are not as they were presented.

CHAPTER 15

Full-blown investigations

Tax investigations are initiated by what is commonly known as a 'Mae West' letter, a letter to the taxpayer inviting him or her to 'come up and see me sometime'.

Formal tax investigations are conducted under what is known as Code of Practice 9 (COP9). This is a civil procedure used when HMRC suspects tax fraud but does not wish to pursue a criminal investigation. The procedure is also known as a Contractual Disclosure Facility (CDF). Cases where HMRC suspects that significantly less tax was declared than should have been the case, although there is no suspicion of fraud (e.g. residence and technical challenges), follow a different procedure, known as Code of Practice 8 (COP8). The opening gambits in this procedure differ from COP9 but thereafter, in the main, the two procedures are basically the same.

Code of Practice 9 opening letter

Dear Mr Frank

HMRC has information that gives it reason to suspect that you have committed tax fraud. I intend to investigate your tax fraud under 'Code of Practice 9 – HMRC investigations where we suspect tax fraud' (COP9). My investigation will cover all of your tax affairs.

COP9 sets out how we investigate suspected fraud and it applies to your tax affairs from the date of this letter. I enclose a copy of COP9. You should read it carefully as it explains everything you need to know before you decide whether to make a disclosure...

Under COP9, as part of a contractual arrangement called the Contractual Disclosure Facility, we offer you the opportunity to make a full disclosure of all tax losses brought about by your deliberate and non-deliberate conduct. If you make a full disclosure under the CDF, we will not start a criminal investigation with a view to prosecution into any deliberate conduct that you disclose.

This CDF will not apply to any other offences which you do not disclose. We may also investigate you with a view to prosecution if you provide false or misleading information, for example deliberately understating the extent of the tax you evaded.

You have 60 days from the date you receive this letter to tell us whether you want to make a disclosure under the CDF or whether you want to reject our offer to make a disclosure.

If after reading this letter and COP9, you have any questions about the CDF process, you should speak to your adviser.

Yours sincerely
HMRC FIS Officer

Investigation process (COP8 and COP9)

Notification letter from HMRC
An investigation starts when HMRC issues an opening letter, as it believes it has cause to investigate you, the taxpayer, or if you volunteer information to HMRC.

Outline disclosure or denial (COP9 only)
You, the taxpayer, have 60 days from the date of HMRC's opening letter to either deny deliberately making mistakes with your tax affairs (i.e. fraud) or to admit them, providing details of all errors and omissions.

Interview (COP9 only)
HMRC interviews you to understand your disclosure in more detail and to obtain more information, e.g. on your lifestyle, dependants and means.

Scoping meeting
Your advisers attend this meeting with HMRC to agree the scope (topics, tax years, etc.) of the disclosure report to be prepared and the deadline for its submission.

Preparation of disclosure report

Your advisers, with your full assistance, prepare a detailed disclosure report, setting out full facts for all errors and omissions, the tax at stake and why the mistakes occurred for submission to HMRC. In COP9 cases, a full bank analysis and means review is often included, too. This takes at least six months, during which progress meetings with HMRC happen periodically. HMRC may also issue 'protective' discovery assessments.

Clarification meeting

After the report's submission, your advisers will usually meet with HMRC at least once to discuss and resolve queries and provisionally agree the tax, interest and penalties payable.

Letter of offer

This is a formal letter to HMRC, signed by you, proposing a figure to settle the case. Occasionally you sign this at a formal settlement meeting with HMRC. If the case is progressing to Tribunal instead, HMRC will issue tax and penalty assessments and the formal appeal process starts.

Acceptance letter

The HMRC officer completes copious paperwork, and your offer progresses through governance reviews. If it succeeds, you receive an acceptance letter formally closing the investigation.

Full-blown investigations start for all sorts of reasons – often due to discrepancies between tax returns and information that Connect analyses (see Chapter 2), or tip-offs supported by other evidence. Occasionally they are triggered by other events. Police found about £50,000 in cash in a raid on a UK house, then satisfied themselves that there was no criminal activity other than unpaid taxes. HMRC opened a COP9 and carried out a detailed review of the owners' income and outgoings, including eight years of Caribbean holidays and expensive cars, before assessing eight years' taxes and penalties. The culprits also were publicly named as deliberate tax defaulters.

Procedures tend to go on a bit – a bit too long for most taxpayers' liking. Part of the reason for this is that they go into great depth, requiring large amounts of information and detailed disclosure reports. At any one time there are probably several thousand investigations that have been running for over three years. Increasingly they involve overseas assets, and this can stretch them into the future. Clearing the cobwebs off overseas banks' records of dividend or interest payments is a time-consuming affair.

The threat of prosecution and a long-running investigation puts enormous stress on individuals who come into HMRC's web. First of all, there is the shame of it – to this day it is not the natural subject of polite dinner-party conversations ('So, when you come back from the Virgin Islands will they lock you up? Would you like another potato?')

The strain is not just on the person under investigation, either. It also falls on their immediate family, not all of whom will see the situation in the same light as the taxpayer. For example, an opportunity to lay claim to part of a hitherto hidden asset may suddenly move a disgruntled partner to action. Moreover, children will not always be on good terms with one another. A brother and sister who were not talking to each other received a call one day to say that their father had died, leaving £10 million in a trust for them in Switzerland. The father had been a bit of a rogue, telling the UK authorities that he lived in Germany, and the German authorities that he lived in the UK. With the help of their advisers, the heirs made a full voluntary disclosure and closed the trust – without either of them ever saying a word to the other.

During an investigation there is always a strong temptation to get it off your chest, to talk too much – to the wrong people and about the wrong things. Once caught in the spider's web, taxpayers tend to thrash about aimlessly in their determination to escape. Unburdening your soul is best done to your adviser, at least in the first instance.

There is absolutely no reason to tell the jolly stranger in the pub about your tax affairs just because you were asked. There are still a few jolly tax officers around (believe it or not), and they like to have a drink in the pub as much as the rest of us. It is best to take note of those World War Two slogans: 'Careless Talk Costs Lives' and 'Silence Means Security' – slogans that have made a curious comeback in the age of social media when, for many, silence seems to be living death.

If a tax officer begins to ask about little Johnny's education, don't believe she is genuinely interested in the future of your tattooed teenage wastrel. She probably wants to know what the fees are at the institution where darling Johnny has been incarcerated since the age of seven ... and where the money to pay those fees has come from.

In many cases, advisers can broadly tell within the first

Full-blown investigations

hour of the first meeting how the case is going to progress. They cannot forecast the actual outcome, of course, but they do get to know the parameters. Attitude is important. It does not pay to be too casual and to act as if you don't know what all the fuss is about.

On the other hand, it is not wise to become aggressive or to lose your temper while under investigation. This is a particular risk for self-made businessmen who are accustomed to getting what they want if they shout loud enough. Throwing a chair across the room in a meeting with HMRC does not create an automatic right to chair the meeting.

Such people tend to see life as a competition in which the winner is the man who finds the cheapest way round obstacles. This, however, is not the aim of a tax investigation, where the only point is to end up with a settlement and without a criminal investigation and/or bankruptcy.

Whatever a taxpayer's attitude to an investigation, it is important to remain fit for the duration. Unhealthy, stressed flies are less likely to escape a spider's web than their fitter counterparts. Taxpayers who do fall ill should get a doctor's certificate to that effect. HMRC is not totally unsympathetic to ill health.

And don't imagine that death is a solution. Although the European Court of Human Rights states that tax penalties cannot be imposed on the living in respect of a person now deceased, HMRC has four years after someone dies in which to check the dead person's returns (and it loves digging up ghosts from the past). If it finds an error, it can reassess liabilities for the six years immediately before his or her death, as well as continuing any enquiries or appeals in progress at his or her demise. The deceased's estate is then liable.

While COP8 investigations only focus on specific problem areas – usually involving tax avoidance or tax planning for which the implementation may not be all that it seems – COP9s are more invasive. FIS will want the taxpayer to disclose all their mistakes and to help satisfy HMRC that there is nothing more to resolve. The officers will compare the information they hold – including the nuggets of gold hidden in

Connect – against the information disclosed by the taxpayer. They will follow through the money involved in transactions to accounting records and bank accounts to check the stories stack up. They also often expect a detailed analysis of bank

Some forms HMRC expects to receive during complex investigations

Certificate of Full Disclosure (CFD)	Certificate confirming that a full disclosure relevant to your UK tax affairs has been made
Statement of Assets and Liabilities	Akin to a personal balance sheet – showing all your assets and liabilities at a particular date or dates
Certificate of Bank and Building Society Accounts	Lists all the bank accounts in your name (including joint accounts) and those on which you had signing powers during a specific period, together with the opening and closing dates
Certificate of Credit Cards	Lists all your credit cards during a specific period, together with the opening and closing dates
Adoption Certificate	Adopts the disclosure report as your full disclosure
Offer letter	Offers HMRC a sum of money to cover tax, interest and penalties to close the investigation – only at the end of the process, after negotiation

account deposits and payments for several years, justification of purchases of assets and completion of standard forms. Together these provide a detailed picture of your finances and any potential black holes.

One taxpayer who signed a Certificate of Full Disclosure did not tell the taxman about his offshore accounts. A couple of years later, his conscience got the better of him and he confessed to having those accounts and owning two horses. It was subsequently discovered that he sold chickens off the back of a lorry and developed properties – all hidden from view. In the course of the investigation a veritable herd of horses suddenly galloped over the horizon, too!

Most investigations end with the issuance of an acceptance letter, a formal document from HMRC declaring that it has accepted the taxpayer's offer and closed its investigation. However, it is never a good idea to jump with joy once you hear the final settlement – you never know who might be watching.

CHAPTER 16

Criminal investigations

Despite the increasing number of strands in HMRC's tangled web, the worst-case scenario for anyone who gets caught up in it remains a rare occurrence. Prison is still an unlikely final destination for the tax offender. In 2017, 762 individuals were sentenced to a total of more than 1,000 years in prison for their part in tax crimes. That's about 15 months each, on average. However, sentences vary greatly, depending on the offence.

Some tax offenders are distinctly more likely than others to end up behind a web of barbed wire: repeat offenders, for example, and lawyers and accountants – people who by the nature of their job ought to know better.

HMRC says it will consider whether a criminal investigation is appropriate 'where there are grounds to believe that evasion is involved'. In this context, evasion means intentionally or recklessly misleading HMRC by failing to supply correct information. It is sometimes paired with the offence of fraud, which occurs when documents are falsified.

Historically it has proved difficult for HMRC to demonstrate in court beyond reasonable doubt that a taxpayer has 'intentionally' got his sums wrong. In certain tax cases,

> **Some criminal offences that may relate to tax**
> - Fraudulent evasion of income tax
> - False accounting
> - Fraud
> - Cheating the public revenue
> - Money laundering
> - Failing to prevent the criminal facilitation of tax evasion

however, where there are 'offshore matters' or 'offshore transfers' involved, the balance can shift in HMRC's favour by the application of the legal concept of 'strict liability'. For strict liability criminal offences, the prosecutor only needs to prove that something has happened (e.g. an incorrect return was submitted, or a return was filed more than two years after the end of the tax year). There is no need to prove intent as well. Those convicted face unlimited fines and/or prison sentences of up to 51 weeks. The only defences are having a 'reasonable excuse' or taking 'reasonable care'.

HMRC's FIS has been described as the 'Premier League' of HMRC investigators, and is staffed by some of its most able and experienced officers. In cases of suspected fraud, it has to decide whether to pursue a criminal prosecution or a civil investigation under COP9. Recently it has been under pressure from Parliament to increase the number of both. To some extent it has succeeded. There were 3,809 criminal investigations into serious tax evasion cases in 2017/18, up from 2,749 cases in 2015.

The number of high-profile offshore cases did not rise proportionately, though, and MPs claim that this sustains 'the impression that the rich can get away with tax fraud'. Consequently, HMRC is homing in on the UK's wealthiest residents – high-net-worth individuals (HNWIs); folks with assets of more than £10 million. By 2020 HMRC is targeted to increase to 100 the number of prosecutions of both HNWIs and corporations that it makes each year.

Often the first the taxpayer knows about a criminal investigation is the knock at the door in the early hours of the morning. This is a raid. The HMRC team will be ably assisted by the police or other agencies, and its web is usually stretched to ensnare victims at multiple locations, such as home, office and warehouse. A search will ensue, during which they may seize documents, computers and phones, and the taxpayer may be arrested, too.

Sometimes the start is a little more benign, taking the form of a brief letter inviting the taxpayer for interview. Regardless of the way it starts, urgent professional advice from an experienced white-collar crime lawyer is essential. Say nothing until this advice arrives.

Another tool to help 'stop the rich getting away with it' is the Unexplained Wealth Order (UWO). This was introduced as part of the Criminal Finances Act 2017. It dramatically reverses the burden of proof. In the past, if suspicious, the State had to prove that a person's money (and the assets it purchased) had not been acquired legally. Now, once a UWO is issued, the tables are turned and the owner of the assets has to prove that the money used to purchase them was clean. The court can even freeze ownership of the asset to stop it being sold while the UWO is in play. The government's stated aim is to make the UK a less attractive destination for 'dirty money' – income and capital gained illegally.

The first such order was issued in March 2018 by the High Court at the request of the National Crime Agency (it could have been at HMRC's request). Issued to a 'politically exposed person', it asked him to prove the source of funds used to buy a £22 million London property. Should he fail to prove that satisfactorily, the State could confiscate the property.

For some years now, the taxman's web has been used to catch more than mere houseflies. Officers occasionally pursue taxpayers with tax evasion charges when they suspect them of more serious crimes because, that way, they have a better chance of getting them behind bars. For obvious reasons these are known as 'Al Capone cases'.

Criminal investigations

The final destination

Having scrabbled our way through the web of HMRC information and investigations, pausing to consider the diversity of taxpayers en route, we reach a point where HMRC is fairly sure how much tax is due. We are nearing the escape from the web, but there are just a few final loose ends to work though. There are usually legal procedures, penalties and payment before we reach the final destination.

CHAPTER 17

Legal procedures

Taxpayers who feel that a ruling by HMRC is incorrect usually have the right to appeal. There is generally a choice – internal review or the Tribunal. Internal reviews are what it says on the tin. The case is handed to a separate officer elsewhere in HMRC who gives it a second look. Sometimes this is all that it takes for 'sense' to prevail, particularly on penalty cases. In 2016/17, more than half HMRC's original decisions were changed or cancelled following internal review.

There are two types of Tribunal – a so-called First-Tier Tribunal (FTT) and an Upper Tribunal. The FTT is the first port of call. Its decisions may then be appealed (usually only on points of law rather than of fact) to the Upper Tribunal. The FTT's judgements do not, however, create a legal precedent, whereas the findings of the Upper Tribunal do. After appealing to the Tribunals, taxpayers still have the right to appeal directly to the courts – if they get permission – although they have not in the past had a great track record there.

Alternatively, if there is no formal right of appeal, they can ask the High Court for a judicial review (JR). If permitted, JR is a procedure in which the courts reconsider decisions made by public bodies such as HMRC – for example, to see if they were illegal, irrational or unreasonable. The number of judicial reviews has risen steadily in recent years, perhaps because HMRC is using new powers, such as Accelerated Payment Notices, against which formal appeals cannot be made.

There is also a process called Alternative Dispute Resolution (ADR). This offers a shortcut for companies and individuals to resolve disputes. ADR is a mediation process in which a trained mediator, who was not previously involved in the case, acts as a go-between. All the action usually takes place on one day. After an initial meeting together, the mediator facilitates discussions by shuttle diplomacy.

ADR offers the possibility of settling stalled disputes in a single day. This is an attractive carrot in many cases. While it is not suitable for all disputes, it is proving effective as it reinvigorates discussions and does not affect the taxpayer's rights of appeal. Sometimes it is amazing how a few hours' discussion can clarify facts or clear the air, unravelling previously entrenched positions, misgivings and misunderstandings so that a mutually acceptable result is possible.

Tips for effective appeals

- Consider your strategy – don't threaten unless you are prepared to go through with it.
- Set out the grounds of your appeal fully, and don't forget to seek postponement of the tax if possible.
- Use internal review unless HMRC's boards or technical specialist is already involved.
- A detailed letter to the review officer setting out your case and explaining your position is advisable at the outset of an internal review.
- Consider ADR – mediation is a powerful tool.
- Preparation is essential – whether for ADR or a Tribunal hearing. The burden of proof is usually on the taxpayer.
- Don't assume – particularly don't assume HMRC will give up at the thought of court, or that the court will anonymise their decision to save your blushes.
- Evidence, evidence, evidence – never underestimate its importance. Also, third-party evidence is best, followed by contemporaneous notes, other people's recollections or your memories. Credible witnesses are essential.
- Meet deadlines – the court sets lots of them and woe betide anyone who misses them.
- Be clear about costs – initially both sides usually pay their own way. Later, loser takes all.

HMRC's taxpayers' charter ('Your Charter') sets out what each taxpayer should expect from HMRC and what HMRC expects of them (see Appendix 4, page 118). Taxpayers who feel aggrieved about the way they have been treated during an investigation (as opposed to the conclusion it reaches) also have the right to complain. There is a standard procedure that allows them to complain to the case worker, complaints manager and, if necessary, an HMRC director – which is sufficient to sort out most cases. Anyone who wants to take matters further can turn to an 'impartial' referee called the Adjudicator, and for those for whom this is not sufficient there is the right to ask an MP to refer their case to the parliamentary ombudsman.

There is a growing feeling that where taxpayers do have a right of appeal, the system is increasingly stacked against them. Once it has won a legal victory in a court in a parallel case, for example, HMRC can demand payment of still-disputed sums by sending out Follower Notices. Combined with the possibility of a 50 per cent penalty if HMRC subsequently wins the case in a higher court, this is enough to discourage many taxpayers from going to appeal. They are further discouraged by the fact that, historically, HMRC has won about 80 per cent of all such cases.

Nevertheless, taxpayers do still manage to win some significant victories. In one recent example, HMRC was roundly criticised for trying to impose an information order on a taxpayer who had been non-resident for over 15 years. And in another case, where a taxpayer was shown to have some undeclared income, HMRC was unable to identify the source of the income and was therefore prohibited from taxing it.

CHAPTER 18

Penalties

The only question many people want answered when they get involved in a tax investigation is 'How much is it going to cost me?' These are the sort of people who want to know the price of everything before they make a decision about anything. But there is no correct answer at the start. The final bill is always, to some extent, at the discretion of the tax officer.

Basically, however, there are three elements to the final settlement:

- The amount of previously unpaid tax;
- The interest on that tax (which can be considerable if it was unpaid for a number of years, as it is an arithmetic computation that aims to put the government back to where it would have been if the tax had been paid on time); and
- The penalties that HMRC will impose, usually calculated as a percentage of the tax (plus flat-rate late-filing penalties).

The first two of these elements are relatively easily quantifiable. The size of the third, the penalty, is dependent on three different things:

- The type of the mistake (error in a tax return, failure to register to pay tax);
- The taxpayer's behaviour in making the understatements; and
- The extent to which the taxpayer was helpful during the investigation – in particular, in pointing a finger at the 'enablers' of whatever avoidance scheme might have been used.

HMRC doesn't often buy into 'innocent' errors. However, it has a list in its 'Compliance Handbook' of situations where it might consider the taxpayer took reasonable care. This may include following advice from HMRC or a professional adviser that later proves to be incorrect, assuming that the advice was not obviously wrong and that full facts were given before the advice was proffered.

Careless errors are what they sound like – errors that are careless. One wealthy man had 25 different bank accounts and forgot to include just one of them in his tax returns one year, as the bank did not send the usual interest certificate. The problem was that the interest on the account was a quarter of a million pounds! The taxman thought he must have known his return was wrong. However, HMRC was eventually persuaded that the client's behaviour was careless and not deliberate. He didn't intend to make the mistake, but he hadn't bothered to double check that he'd got all the certificates before giving them to his accountant. The account was relatively new, too, so the accountant didn't realise either.

Where there has been a deliberate attempt to deceive, though, HMRC comes down hard. The number of deliberate behaviour penalties imposed increased by 19 per cent in 2016/17 (to 34,100) compared to the previous year. Coincidentally, over the same period there was a decline in the number of penalties for carelessness. Since there is no evidence to suggest that the British taxpayer has become less careless and more deceitful over that period, it seems as if HMRC has moved the goalposts or its expectations of taxpayers. Some of what is now considered deliberate was once seen as careless – which has a positive effect on the taxman's take, since the penalties for mere carelessness are generally lower.

Penalties for documents sent to HMRC, such as tax returns or claims, that are found to contain errors are calculated using the behaviour bandings shown in the graph overleaf (see also Appendix 5, page 119).

As you can see, lower penalties are possible if the taxpayer voluntarily bears all and makes an unprompted disclosure (see Chapter 5). The penalties are often higher if there are offshore issues (see Appendix 6, page 121); HMRC penalises mistakes relating to offshore matters rather more, as they are generally a bit harder to find and investigate. Similar penalties exist for

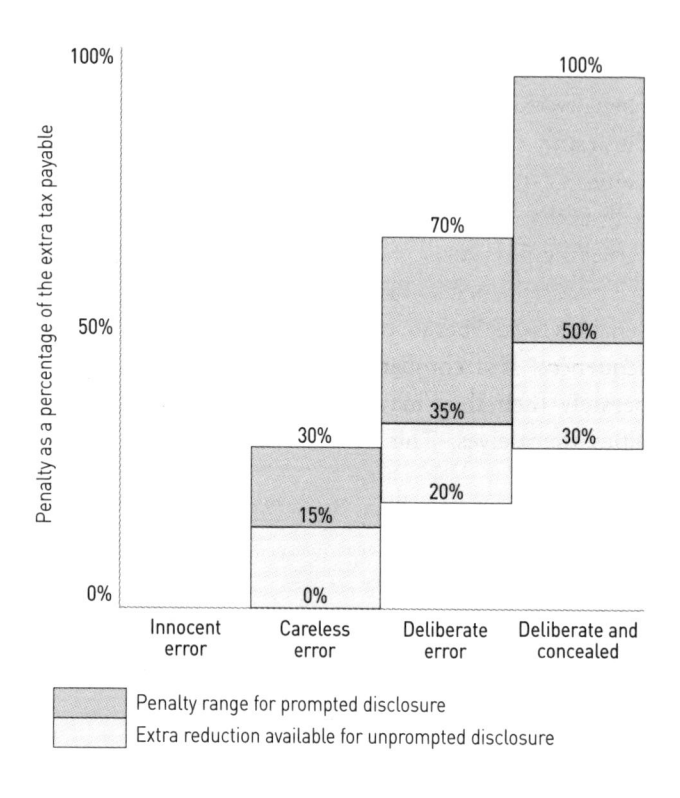

Bar chart: Penalty as a percentage of the extra tax payable

Category	Penalty range for prompted disclosure	Extra reduction available for unprompted disclosure
Innocent error	0%	—
Careless error	15%–30%	0%–15%
Deliberate error	35%–70%	20%–35%
Deliberate and concealed	50%–100%	30%–50%

failures to notify HMRC that tax returns need to be filed, for which the 'get out of jail free' card is having a 'reasonable excuse', or for deliberately withholding information by filing some types of returns more than 12 months late.

HMRC has discretion to reduce the penalties, depending on the existence of any special circumstances and its judgement of the 'quality' of the disclosure – was it given in full at the first opportunity, for example, or did it come after the taxpayer's feet had been dunked in a bucket of lethal arachnids, metaphorically speaking?

HMRC likes to change taxpayers' behaviour where possible. The penalty regime offers a perfect opportunity, particularly for those scared of meeting spiders.

Careless error penalties may be suspended for up to two years in exchange for the taxpayer agreeing to take steps to avoid making careless errors in future. If the suspension conditions are met, the penalty is never payable.

Penalties for deliberate behaviour come with more serious consequences. If a company's directors made the mistakes deliberately then they may have to pay part or all of the penalties themselves. Third parties who deliberately cause

---

Penalty reductions depend on the timing, nature and extent of the following categories. Maximum reductions are:

Telling HMRC about the issue and why it arose	30%
Helping HMRC quantify the tax liability	40%
Giving HMRC access to records to check the accuracy of the disclosure	30%
	100%

Where someone takes a 'significant' period (usually over three years) to correct their mistake, or they could previously have made a disclosure through an offshore disclosure facility, HMRC will restrict the maximum reduction for the quality of disclosure by 10 percentage points.

others to file incorrect returns will also pay the price. HMRC has a subset of deliberate defaulters that it calls 'serious defaulters'. These taxpayers' affairs are monitored closely for at least two years after they are exposed to ensure they are now behaving themselves.

Most scary of all is public notification of being entangled in HMRC's investigations web and punished for deliberate mistakes. If the tax at stake exceeds £25,000 then HMRC can publish the person's name, address, tax and penalties on the government website for 12 months.

In one recently published naming and shaming of 'deliberate defaulters', a second-hand car salesman who owed tax of £26,740 was charged a penalty of £15,288, and a scrap-metal dealer was charged 100 per cent of the amount due (as well as the amount due).

In an attempt to put additional pressure on offshore tax evaders HMRC will only permit taxpayers who voluntarily confessed their sins and obtained the minimum penalty to escape the public shaming. To add extra pressure, HMRC requires taxpayers to tell it who helped them evade tax before HMRC will consider giving them the maximum penalty mitigation.

This is a new rule so we may have to wait a few years before we find out whether this turns the UK into a nation of snitches, or whether people will pay more to protect their friends, and so on. HMRC, however, hopes the cash saving will encourage people to help them with their enquiries and provide them with candidates for investigation for the criminal offence of facilitating offshore tax evasion or the civil sanctions of enabling offshore non-compliance.

CHAPTER 19

Tax debt management

HMRC has made it perfectly clear that lacking available cash is not normally a reasonable excuse for not paying taxes. On the contrary, taxpayers would be well advised to make significant (but relevant) payments on account whenever possible, selling assets when needs be. HMRC sees this as an important sign of a willingness to cooperate. It may also save the taxpayer a large amount of interest, since interest accrues from the date on which the tax should have been paid through to the day when it is actually paid. This does, of course, depend on the prevailing rate of interest.

Taxpayers who have genuine difficulty in paying their tax on time can apply to pay by instalments through direct debits. The interest will be adjusted accordingly. Often this also means late payment penalties are avoided if the arrangement is agreed in advance.

HMRC has the right to demand that taxpayers pay a deposit in advance (as security) on unpaid tax when it thinks there is a risk that the tax will not be forthcoming. These 'security deposits' can then be offset against future tax payments, e.g. of PAYE, NIC and VAT. Failure to provide security for tax debts is a criminal offence.

Usually when an appeal to the FTT is ongoing, direct tax is put on ice – postponed. VAT must be paid nonetheless, unless this causes hardship. Sometimes HMRC refuses the ice bucket and demands payment regardless. This may result in bankruptcy (for individuals) or liquidation (for companies) if their tax appeal lacks merit.

HMRC has a right to seize individuals' movable assets should their unpaid tax not be forthcoming. Once enforcement action is taken, bailiffs walk in and possess goods up to the value of the unpaid tax. There are some assets, however, that they cannot lay their hands on. These include the tools of a person's trade, the basic necessities of life, and perishable goods. Hence, since chilled food cannot be taken, neither can a refrigerator. Most taxpayers who reach this point, however, find that fact to be cold comfort.

Under certain circumstances, HMRC can take money directly from a taxpayer's bank account with the bank's assistance. The account will be frozen for a fortnight or more while the procedures are completed – not good if wages have to be paid... Sticking your head in the sand will not mean the problem no longer exists.

Don't think that you can escape HMRC's web by going overseas, either. HMRC has mutual assistance agreements so that certain other countries collect UK tax debts for HMRC and vice versa.

Finally, the tax debts of a company may be transferred from the company to the directors in some circumstances. This also applies to penalties for deliberate errors. The spider's many arms are capable of piercing the corporate veil...

CHAPTER 20

The final destination

HMRC's reinvigorated determination to tackle offshore tax evasion and non-compliance is not yet showing through in the prosecution figures. There are none of the high-profile cases that politicians are longing for; *pour décourager les autres*. The taxman's top ten criminal cases, which it publishes annually, reads like a list of the usual slightly grubby suspects – alcohol and cigarette smugglers, landlords who let property to tenants on (government-funded) housing benefits and then fail to pay any tax on their income. The list is short on heavy hitters from new technology businesses, for example, or from offshore centres. This may all change with the introduction of the strict liability criminal offences and flood of data from overseas courtesy of the Common Reporting Standard (CRS).

There is no doubt that there has been a big shift within HMRC in recent years. The consequences of mistakes are more serious than ever, with penalties potentially exceeding 300 per cent of the tax, plus public shaming of deliberate defaulters. Advisers face severe consequences of enabling errors, too. The government and HMRC hope all this will encourage good behaviour. Time will tell, but the complexity of the rules and lack of adequate publicity may mean this goal is somewhat ambitious, at least in the short term.

HMRC was directed to rein in offshore tax mistakes of all types, as well as cracking down on the use of tax avoidance schemes. It formalised its procedures in a way that allows less room to consider each individual taxpayers' particular circumstances. The consequences of this are as yet unknown.

In the process, old understandings about what is legal and what is not have been somewhat undermined. Taxpayers are understandably confused and more in need of advice than ever. Regardless of the pontifications of politicians, none of us wants to pay more tax than we absolutely have to. This will not change. Perhaps not surprisingly, voluntary restitution is hardly ever offered!

Irrespective of the colour and shade of any future government, HMRC will remain determined to expand its web, and tighten its grip on those who become ensnared in it. We too must keep pace with such change and ensure that taxpayers' rights are fully respected and protected.

Incy Wincy spider climbed up the water spout
Down came the rain and washed the spider out
Out came the sun and dried up all the rain
And Incy Wincy spider climbed up the spout again!

The final destination

APPENDIX 1

Top ten tips

1. Keep calm and don't panic;
2. Get expert advice at the outset;
3. Don't discuss your tax affairs with anyone but a small circle of tax advisers;
4. Don't lie to HMRC;
5. Don't assume HMRC is ignorant of anything;
6. Be well prepared for meetings;
7. Make significant (but relevant) payments on account;
8. Don't try to destroy evidence – digital or otherwise;
9. Never make a partial disclosure;
10. Once you have reached a settlement, don't offend again.

APPENDIX 2

Our ten favourite excuses

'I couldn't file my return on time because my wife has been seeing aliens and won't let me enter the house.'

'My ex-wife left my tax return upstairs, but I suffer from vertigo and can't go to retrieve it.'

'God told me to transfer the shares.'

'My laptop broke, and so did my washing machine.'

'I was up a mountain in Wales and couldn't get on the web.'

'My husband ran over my laptop.'

'I had an argument with my wife and went to Italy for five years.'

'My tax return was on my yacht, which caught fire.'

'A wasp in my car caused me to have an accident and my tax return, which was inside, was destroyed.'

'My wife helps me with my tax return, but she had a headache for ten days.'

APPENDIX 3

UK Statutory Residence Test summary

STEP 1: Conclusive tests

If you say yes to any of these then you are not resident in the UK this year:

- Not UK resident in all 3 previous years and fewer than 46 days in the UK in the current tax year?
- UK resident in one or more of 3 previous tax years and fewer than 16 days in the UK in the current tax year?
- Works abroad full-time and fewer than 91 days in the UK and, of those, fewer than 31 days working in the UK in the current tax year?

If you are not already non-resident from the above tests and you can say yes to any of these three statements, then you are UK resident:

- Spent 183 days or more in the UK in the current tax year
- Your only home is in the UK and you visited that home in the current tax year on 30 or more days (or UK home and overseas home but visits to overseas home minimal)
- Works in sufficient hours in the UK (see definitions)

STEP 2: If Step 1 is inconclusive, determine arriver or leaver status before counting UK ties and UK days in a tax year.

Arriver: not resident in the UK in any of 3 previous tax years
Leaver: UK resident in one or more of the 3 previous tax years

How many UK ties do you have?

- Spouse/civil partner/cohabitee or minor child resident in the UK
- Accommodation available in the UK for 91 days or more in the tax year and at least one night spent there
- Work (3 hours or more) in the UK on 40 or more days in the tax year
- More than 90 days in the UK in either of the two previous tax years
- More 'midnights' in the UK than in any other country (leavers only)

Residency test:

Arrivers	Days in UK in tax year	Leavers
Not resident	0–15	Not resident
Not resident	16–45	Resident if 4 ties
Resident if 4 ties	46–90	Resident if 3 ties
Resident if 3 ties	91–120	Resident if 2 ties
Resident if 2 ties	121–182	Resident if 1 tie
Resident	183 or more	Resident

For example, if a UK leaver's wife and children remain resident here, there is available UK accommodation and the 90-day test is met, then the leaver can spend up to 45 days in the UK before becoming resident.

Key definitions:

- **A day** in the UK at midnight is counted (apart from working day tests). However, if you are just in transit and do no other activity here (e.g. meetings) then you ignore the day. Days may be ignored in exceptional circumstances.

- **Full-time work overseas:** You must work sufficient hours, which broadly equates to 35 hours per week on average per year, with no significant break of 31 days or more where you work less than 3 hours a day.

- **Works sufficient hours in the UK:** You must work sufficient hours in the UK over a 365-day period (broadly, an average of 35 hours per week) with no significant breaks from UK work. More than 75% of the days in the period when you work for more than 3 hours per day must be in the UK and you must work in the UK for more than 3 hours on at least one day in the current tax year.

- **Workdays:** A UK work day for the SRT is a day on which more than 3 hours' work is performed. Work includes incidental and non-incidental duties and most travel.

- **Home:** 'a building (or part of a building), a vehicle, vessel or structure of any kind which is used as a home or dwelling by an individual.' You do not need to own the home but it does not include somewhere only used periodically (e.g. a holiday home, temporary retreat, property being advertised for sale or let where the individual lives somewhere else).

- **Accommodation:** a place to live – can include a holiday or weekend home or a hotel room (where staying for at least one night) or a relative's home (if the individual stays there for 16 nights or more in the tax year).

- **Visits:** individuals 'use' a home they own on a day if they spend any time there (however short, presence at midnight is not required).

- **Tax year:** 6 April one year to 5 April in the following year.

- **Part days rule for leavers with 3 or 4 ties only:** includes the number of days in the tax year for which the individual was present in the UK for some part of the day but left the UK before midnight – but deduct the first 30 days.

This is a summary of the rules. It does not cover all circumstances and should not be relied upon. Specific advice should be sought from an expert in this area.

Arrivers: Simple scenarios	Simple solutions
Husband & wife have a UK house; neither work in the UK	They can always spend 120 days/tax year in the UK without becoming resident
Husband & wife have a UK house; both work in the UK	They can always spend 90 days/tax year in the UK without becoming resident
Husband & wife have a UK house; he works and she does not	He can spend 90 days; she can spend 120 days/tax year in the UK without becoming resident
Individual has UK house and UK work	They can spend up to 120 days in the UK one year in three and up to 90 days otherwise without becoming UK resident

Tax impact of UK residence

Status of individual		Income		Capital gains		Inheritance tax	
		UK source	Non-UK source	UK assets	Non-UK assets	UK assets	Non-UK assets
Domiciled or deemed domiciled	Resident	Taxable as arises	Taxable as arises	Taxable as arises	Taxable as arises	Taxable	Taxable
	Non-resident	Taxable as arises	Not liable to UK tax[1]	Not liable to UK tax[1,2]	Not liable to UK tax[1]	Taxable	Taxable
Non-domiciled (remittance basis and not UK deemed domiciled)	Resident	Taxable as arises	Taxable if remitted	Taxable as arises	Taxable if remitted	Taxable	Not liable to tax
	Non-resident	Taxable as arises	Not liable to tax[1]	Not liable to tax[1,2]	Not liable to tax[1]	Taxable	Not liable to tax

[1] May be taxable on return if only temporarily non-UK resident

[2] Sales of UK residential property will be within the scope of UK CGT when owned by any person, regardless of residence or domicile status.

This is a summary of the rules. It does not cover all circumstances and should not be relied upon. Specific advice should be sought from an expert in this area.

APPENDIX 4

HMRC's taxpayer's charter

Your Charter

We want to give you a service that is fair, accurate and based on mutual trust and respect. We also want to make it as easy as we can for you to get things right.

'Your Charter' explains what you can expect from us and what we expect from you.

Your rights – what you can expect from us:	Your obligations – what we expect from you:
Respect you and treat you as honest	Be honest and respect our staff
Provide a helpful, efficient and effective service	Work with us to get things right
Be professional and act with integrity	Find out what you need to do to keep us informed
Protect your information and respect privacy	Keep accurate records and protect your information
Accept that someone else can represent you	Know what your representative does on your behalf
Deal with complaints quickly and fairly	Respond in good time
Tackle those who bend or break the rules	Take reasonable care to avoid mistakes

Source: www.gov.uk/government/publications/your-charter/your-charter

APPENDIX 5

Behaviours

Reasonable care	Taking proper care to submit a correct tax return but making a mistake nonetheless, e.g. – By making a small transposition or arithmetical error; – Relying on information from a third party that you cannot check and that later proves to be incorrect; or – Relying on professional advice that appears not to be obviously wrong, after giving the adviser the full facts.
Reasonable excuse	An excuse that is reasonable in the circumstances. Ignorance is rarely a reasonable excuse.
Careless	Failure to take reasonable care (i.e. negligence) when submitting a document such as a tax return; or The mistake was not careless or deliberate when the document was submitted but the taxpayer discovered the error some time later and did not take reasonable steps to inform HMRC; or The mistake relates to a defeated tax avoidance arrangement and is deemed careless by the legislation.

▶

Behaviours continued

Non-deliberate failure	Unintentional failure to do something for which you do not have a reasonable excuse.
Deliberate	A mistake or failure that was intentional, e.g. – Intentionally providing HMRC with a tax return despite knowing that it contains errors or omits taxable income; or – Consciously neglecting to find out the correct position (e.g. whether you need to file a tax return) despite knowing that you should do so.
Deliberate & concealed	A deliberate error or mistake that was hidden, for example by using false invoices or by using a bank account that was in a different name.

APPENDIX 6

Penalties for offshore matters and offshore transfers

Some or all of the following penalties may apply:

Offshore penalty 'uplifts' – the standard penalties in the graph on page 98 increase, depending on the country in which the offshore income, assets or profits were located. The maximum penalties are twice those shown on the graph. The minimum penalties increase, too.

More effort needed to mitigate penalties – for tax years from April 2017, additional information must be provided to maximise penalty reductions. Additional information includes details of anyone else with whom you own the assets and details of anyone who encouraged, assisted or facilitated your offshore non-compliance.

Failure to correct penalties – the standard penalty rules with offshore uplifts are replaced by 'failure to correct' penalties, which are 100–200% of the tax (regardless of the behaviour causing the mistake) if the taxpayer failed to correct their UK tax position by 30 September 2018 for years to 5 April 2016 without a reasonable excuse for that failure.

Offshore asset moves penalties (OAMPs) – These are charged in addition to deliberate behaviour penalties if the taxpayer moves themselves or their assets from a country adopting CRS reporting to one that does not ▶

report under CRS with the intention of keeping funds hidden from HMRC. OAMPs are 50% of the standard tax-geared penalty percentage inclusive of any offshore uplifts.

Asset-based penalties – additional penalty of the lower of 10% of the value of the asset and 10 times the extra taxable income or gains that arose due to the mistake.

Glossary of acronyms (and more)

Acceptance letter
A letter sent by HMRC to a taxpayer, indicating that an investigation or a process of voluntary disclosure has come to a satisfactory conclusion – i.e. all unpaid tax, interest and penalties are agreed.

ADR – Alternative Dispute Resolution
A mediation process in which a trained mediator, who has not up to that point been involved in the case, acts as a go-between in a disputed tax case.

APN – Accelerated Payment Notice
A demand for a payment on account of the amount that HMRC believes is attributable to the tax advantage a taxpayer obtained from a tax avoidance scheme. The taxpayer may be corporate or individual – if a partnership, then each partner is issued with a Partner Payment Notice.

ATED – Annual Tax on Enveloped Dwellings

BEPS – base erosion and profit shifting
The artificial shifting of profits from a high-tax jurisdiction to a low-tax one.

CDF – Contractual Disclosure Facility
See COP9

CGT – Capital gains tax

Compliance check
A check by HMRC of a taxpayer's tax position – informally or by using formal civil powers – to ensure they pay 'the right amount of tax at the right time and receive the right allowances and tax reliefs'.

COP8 – Code of Practice 8
The procedure followed by HMRC in civil cases where it suspects that significantly less tax was disclosed than should have been but where there is no suspicion of fraud.

COP9 – Code of Practice 9
A civil procedure used when HMRC suspects tax fraud but does not wish to pursue a criminal investigation. The procedure is also known as a Contractual Disclosure Facility (CDF).

CRS – Common Reporting Standard
An international agreement whereby financial institutions in around 100 different jurisdictions are compelled to pass to their tax authorities certain information about the income of customers who are resident in other countries. The tax authorities of the participating jurisdictions then share the information with any overseas authority in which the customer is based. The USA did not adopt the CRS, choosing to stick with its version, the Foreign Account Tax Compliance Act (FATCA).

Discovery enquiry
There is no such process in law. However this is, in effect, what happens if HMRC uses a combination of its information-gathering powers and its power to issue discovery assessments

to charge tax for past years when there is no formal open self assessment enquiry.

DOTAS – Disclosure of Tax Avoidance Schemes
A requirement that the promoter of certain types of avoidance scheme should disclose that scheme to the tax authorities up front. Having a DOTAS number is not like having a gold star – it is no guarantee of the scheme's success or HMRC's approval. Not surprisingly, the rules on this one are fiendishly complicated. The web thickens.

DPT – Diverted Profits Tax
Introduced in 2015, this imposes a 25 per cent charge on companies deemed to be artificially shifting profits overseas. The stated aim is to 'counter the use of aggressive tax-planning techniques by multinational enterprises to divert profits from the UK to low-tax jurisdictions'.

Enquiry
A self assessment enquiry is a check of one year's self assessment tax return. The enquiry may focus on one or more specific matters, or may be a full enquiry into the whole tax return and the taxpayer's finances for that year.

Final (and partial) closure notices
Once HMRC has finished a tax enquiry it will issue a closure notice. That can come in two shapes – a final closure notice, which is issued when all points are settled, or a partial closure notice, which brings down the curtain on certain outstanding issues, but not all of them.

FIS – Fraud Investigation Service
A specialist team of HMRC officers formed in 2015 to streamline the investigation of civil and criminal cases.

FN – Follower Notices
Notices requiring that taxpayers whose tax avoidance arrangements are under investigation 'follow' other parallel judicial decisions, or risk large penalties should they continue to argue their arrangements work.

FTT – First-Tier Tribunal
The first port of call for taxpayers wishing to appeal against a decision by HMRC. The FTT's decisions can be appealed against (usually only on points of law, rather than fact) to the Upper Tribunal. The FTT's judgements do not create a legal precedent, whereas the findings of the Upper Tribunal do.

GAAR – General Anti-Abuse Rule
Introduced in 2013, the GAAR was designed to give HMRC greater power to counteract 'tax advantages arising from tax arrangements that are abusive'. To be abusive, arrangements have to go 'beyond anything which could reasonably be regarded as a reasonable course of action'. Not to be confused with Targeted Anti-Avoidance Rules (TAARs), which apply to specific tax rules.

Hansard
Hansard is the transcripts that report proceedings of both the House of Commons and the House of Lords.

HMRC – HM Revenue & Customs

HNWI – high-net-worth individual
These are wealthy people with assets worth more than £10 million. Their tax affairs – which are necessarily more complex than the average person's – are dealt with by HMRC's WMBC team (Wealthy Mid-Sized Business Compliance). The specialist team has a better understanding of these affairs and of the specific behaviour of HNWIs.

IHT – inheritance tax

Investigation
A full-blown, in-depth investigation, usually under Code of Practice 8 or 9, but may be a criminal investigation with a view to prosecution in one or more taxes.

JR – judicial review
A challenge in the courts to HMRC's handling of a case, to establish whether HMRC was illegal, irrational or unreasonable.

LSS – Litigation and Settlement Strategy
HMRC's strategy for handling enquiries and investigations. It also sets out when it may reach settlements with taxpayers and when it will litigate.

OCU – Offshore Coordination Unit
Part of the FIS, the Birmingham-based arm of HMRC set up to manage the information that the authority regularly receives from sources around the globe. It deals with most cases involving foreign income and capital.

Offer letter
An offer made by a taxpayer to HMRC of a sum of money to

cover unpaid tax, interest and penalties. The letter is presented only at the end of a process of negotiation and, if HMRC accepts it, then the investigation is brought to a close.

Offshore matter

This is one of the triggers for enhanced sanctions for failures and errors (see Appendix 6, page 121). An offshore matter is a tax liability that is charged on or by reference to income arising, assets situated or activities carried on in a territory outside the UK.

Offshore transfer

This is another trigger for enhanced sanctions for errors and failures (see Appendix 6, page 121). A tax liability involves an offshore transfer if:

- It does not involve an offshore matter;
- It is deliberate; and
- Part or all of the income, gains or disposition by reference to which the tax is charged is received in or transferred to a territory outside the UK.

PAYE – Pay as You Earn

A collection method where employers deduct income tax at source from an employee's salary and pay it to HMRC.

PDDD – Publishing of Deliberate Defaulters' Details

Colloquially known as 'naming and shaming'. Affects taxpayers who are charged tax-geared penalties for deliberate behaviour relating to tax exceeding £25,000. Their details are published on HMRC's website, where they remain for 12 months.

PSC – People with Significant Control
Companies House maintains the UK's PSC register for companies and LLPs. A PSC is an individual who meets one or more of the following conditions:

- Holds more than 25% of a company's shares/LLP's assets on a winding up
- Holds more than 25% of voting rights
- Holds the right to appoint or remove the majority of the board of directors/LLP management
- Has the right to exercise or actually exercises significant influence or control over the company/LLP
- Has the right to exercise or actually exercises significant influence or control over a trust or firm which itself meets one of the above four criteria.

RTC – Requirement to Correct
An obligation on taxpayers to fully disclose any failures or tax return errors relating to offshore matters and offshore transfers that are taxable in the UK.

SAR – Suspicious Activity Report
Any tax adviser who suspects that a client may be involved in money laundering or financing terrorism must file an SAR with the National Crime Agency.

STAR – Serial Tax Avoidance Regime
Rules applied to taxpayers who took advantage of TAAs (see below) that have been 'defeated' (in a court or elsewhere) after 5 April 2017. A curious use of language here by HMRC since STAR can be applied to taxpayers who are participating in only one TAA: a bit like a serial killer who has killed only one person.

TAA – tax avoidance arrangements
An arrangement that tries to use tax legislation to gain a tax advantage that was not intended by Parliament. Ouch!

Tax investigation
This is a full-blown, in-depth investigation, usually carried out under the rules of COP8 or COP9 (see above). It can sometimes, however, be a criminal investigation started with a view to prosecution.

UWO – Unexplained Wealth Order
Introduced as part of the Criminal Finances Act of 2017, an order demanding that the owner of assets prove that the money used to purchase the assets was 'clean'. It dramatically reverses the burden of proof.

WDF – Worldwide Disclosure Facility
A voluntary disclosure facility for offshore issues. It provides no amnesty or reductions of tax, late-payment interest or penalties – although taxpayers who make a full voluntary disclosure are unlikely to face a criminal investigation.

NOTES

NOTES

NOTES

NOTES

NOTES

NOTES

NOTES

NOTES

NOTES

NOTES

NOTES

NOTES